Assignment
in the
Philippines

Assignment in the Philippines

by
Jared Barker

as told to
Marti Hefley

MOODY PRESS
CHICAGO

© 1984 by
THE MOODY BIBLE INSTITUTE
OF CHICAGO

Library of Congress Cataloging in Publication Data

Barker, Jared.
  Assignment in the Philippines.

  1. Barker, Jared. 2. Barker, Marilee. 3. Missionar-
ies—Philippines—Biography. 4. Missionaries—
United States—Biography. 5. Missions—Philippines.
I. Hefly, Marti. II. Title.
BV3382.A1B37   266'.0092'2 [B]   84-8946
ISBN: 0-8024-0265-8

Maps were prepared by Felipe A. Fernandez

1 2 3 4 5 6 7 Printing EB Year 89 88 87 86 85 84

Printed in the United States of America

Contents

CHAPTER   PAGE

Maps of Mindanao and the Philippines   6, 7

1. 4-F   9

2. Real Missionaries   21

3. "We Can Do It!"   37

4. The Barker Hotel   51

5. Opportunities Unlimited   67

6. Troubles and Trials   77

7. Home Is Where the Heart Is   89

8. Patience   97

9. Accepting What I Can't Understand   109

10. Living with Fear   119

11. God Is Faithful   131

12. Servants for Christ   145

MAP OF MINDANAO

LOCATION OF PEEI PROJECTS—

I. MARBEL, KORONADAL

- MISSION HEADQUARTERS
- KING'S COLLEGE
- KING'S FARM
- KING'S CHURCH
- RADIO STATION DXKI

II. ISULAN

- KING'S COLLEGE

III. LAKE SEBU—T'BOLI TRIBE

- KING'S ELEMENTARY SCHOOL
- AGRICULTURE PROJECT
- MEDICAL OUTREACH
- CHURCHES
- FISH PROJECT

IV. LAGUBANG—MANOBO TRIBE

- KING'S ELEMENTARY SCHOOL
- AGRICULTURE
- MEDICAL OUTREACH
- CHURCHES
- DEVELOPMENT PROGRAM

V. LUTAYAN

- FARM PROJECT
- MOSLEM OUTREACH

MISAMIS ORIENTAL

CAGAYAN DE

DIPOLOG CITY

OROQUIETA

MISAMIS OCCIDENTAL

ILIGAN CITY

OGAMIG CITY

LANAO DEL NORTE

MARAWI CITY

ZAMBOANGA DEL NORTE

ZAMBOANGA

PAGADIAN

LANAO LAKE

LANAO DEL SUR

ZAMBOANGA DEL SUR

COTABATO CITY

MAGUINDANAO

NORTH COTABATO

ZAMBOANGA CITY

MORO GULF

LAGUBANG

SULTAN KUDARAT

TACURONG

ISULAN

LAKE BU

LU

COTAB

MAR

KORONADA

BASILAN

SOUTH COTA

SURALLAH

LAKE SEBU

NORTH

CELEBES SEA

10 0 10 20 30 40 50 60 70 80 90 100
KILOMETERS

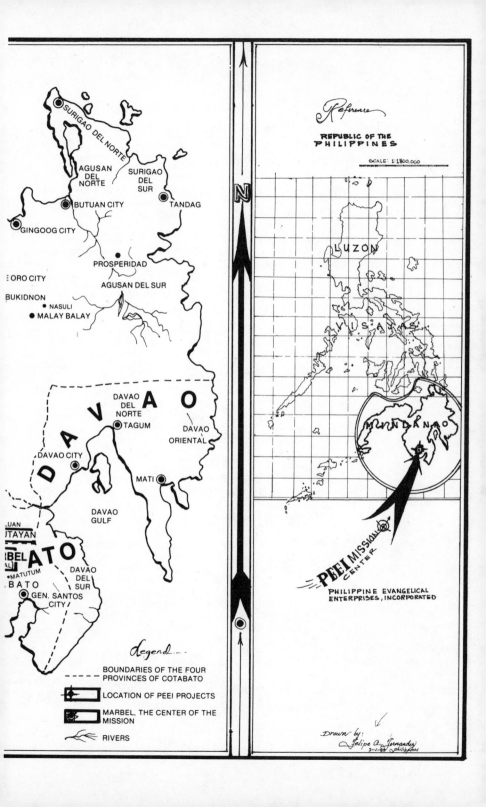

1
"4-F"

"I'm four-F," I announced, flopping down into an easy chair.

"Four-F?" my father repeated incredulously. It was obvious that Bill Barker never expected one of his sons to be an Army reject.

I slouched down in the chair and contemplated my outstretched feet. "The sergeant at Fort Leavenworth said I was unfit for duty because I have *pes planus* third degree."

"What does that mean?"

"Flat feet."

He choked back his laughter and replied solemnly, "Then you'll serve your country here on the farm, Jared. Our soldiers will have to be fed. That will be our part in the war effort."

"But, Dad, the whole graduating class of 'forty-one is enlisting! Uncle Sam wants everyone but me. It's hard to feel very patriotic about farming."

"Life doesn't always deal glamorous tasks to everyone, son. It's going to take the whole country pulling together to win this war. We each have to do our part. Teamwork, that's what's needed."

My father was always more a man of work than of words, so I considered his advice thoughtfully. The war was going to mean a postponement of his dream of a family farm run by himself and his three sons. Only a year before he had lost his farm in Louisburg despite years of back-breaking work. He was now renting a whole section of land near Stanley, Kansas—640 acres of the best land in the county.

Since I wouldn't be serving in the Army I knew they would call up my older brother, Lawrence, and that made me feel bad because he had just married. Little Gene was only ten years old, and he was more of a pest than a help. My two older sisters were away working as radio operators for Northwest Airlines. There was no one else to help Dad, so I figured I might as well stop feeling sorry for myself.

"OK, Dad," I finally agreed with a long sigh, "we'll work the farm together. It'll be rough for just the two of us, but we'll manage somehow."

Dad didn't say anything, but there was something in the proud nod of his head that demonstrated better than words that he approved of me.

My dad had taken me out in the fields to "work" with him before I even started school. He'd let me ride on the old steel-wheeled tractor while he walked along beside me. The tractor only ran two or three miles per hour, but I thought I was driving, and I loved it.

We worked hard during those war years. The day began with milking cows at five o'clock. After a couple of hours of chores I'd work up a tremendous appetite. For breakfast there would be steak and gravy and biscuits with homemade butter and jam. My mother's round face beamed with satisfaction as she watched us packing away the mounds of food she prepared.

While we worked off the morning meal in the fields, she baked bread, cinnamon rolls, cakes, and pies. She also cared for the poultry, gathered eggs, dressed chickens, and tended the kitchen garden. Everyone works on a farm.

There were times I'd have to work thirty-six hours straight—all day, all night, and all the next day. The worst shortage we faced was the lack of manpower, and when a crop is ready to be harvested, it has to be done. Besides, there is a real satisfaction at having a good harvest. I rode our International Harvester Farmall-M tractor with its fifty-horsepower engine through the flowing fields of wheat with a sense of real joy. The fresh, clean smell of newly harvested grain can be delightfully intoxicating.

But by the time the war was over I was ready for a change. Lawrence came marching home, and he and his wife moved in. Gene was a strapping young man by then, well able to put in a good day's work. I felt it was time for me to go to college.

"You're right, Jared. Your education has been interrupted long enough," Dad agreed. "As soon as the fall harvest is over, you can enroll at Kansas State. You need to learn all you can so the four of us can make this the best farm in the state."

Dad was riding high. He believed his dreams were all about to come true. He wanted our farm to be well diversified, and since he loved beef cattle he was pleased that my interests ran more to mechanized farming. I chose the Agricultural Engineering course at K State and enrolled with a bit of trepidation. I was nearly twenty-two years old.

When I arrived on campus I was greatly relieved to find that most of the new students were there under the GI bill. Their educations had been interrupted also. The enrollment jumped from fifteen hundred to three thousand, and the school administration was overwhelmed by the inundation of students. One of the biggest problems was housing, so I was excited when I spotted a sign just across from the campus that read: Vacancy—Male Boarder.

I was met at the door by a blond young philosopher wearing thick glasses. "I'm Bob Milburn," he introduced himself. "I board here. The landlady and her son are out back with their Irish setters. C'mon in. I'll take you to them."

Bob proved to be a very personable fellow, and he negotiated me into moving in. The room wasn't much, and many of the other boarders smoked and smelled up the place. I'd still have to eat the sissy food offered in the cafeteria—salads, lettuce, jello, and little finger foods I consider fit only for women at tea parties.

I was about to walk across the campus for lunch one day when Bob corralled me and insisted, "C'mon, Barker. We're going to pray."

Pray? I thought. *He's going to pray instead of eating? What kind of fanatic is he?*

He overrode my feeble protests and hustled me along to the Religious Activities Building, where we joined eight or ten other students, mostly girls. "Let's pray," someone said, and they all knelt down by their chairs. What else could I do? I knelt too. While I was looking around I noticed the priest and rabbi walking down the hall toward their offices. They looked at us as if we were a bunch of lunatics. They could at least have closed the door!

The students took turns praying one after another in sequence. As the girl next to me started praying I could feel the sweat breaking out on my brow in spite of the chill in the room. I'd never prayed out loud in my life. When she stopped, I took a deep breath and mumbled something I hoped sounded pious. Then Bob, kneeling at my side, started praying for me—that I would come to know Christ as my Savior. I guess I had flunked Prayer 101 or something. It was really embarrassing, but when it was over everyone seemed very open and friendly. No one treated me as an outsider, and they even invited me to come back.

Besides the prayer meetings, Bob invited me to a little rented storefront building down the block a bit from our boardinghouse where a sort of youth center had been established. There were games to play, refreshments, and just clean fun. I didn't fit in with these rather fanatical Christians, but I felt more comfortable with them than with the heavy-smoking, hard-drinking womanizers who lived in the house. Some of those guys had been around a little too much for a country boy like myself.

During the spring semester they invited an evangelist named Bob Finley for a series of meetings at the youth center. He was supposed to be a well-known preacher who traveled the circuit of the newly formed Inter-Varsity group. I'd never heard of him but went to one of the meetings just to check him out.

I expected Finley to be a polished, sophisticated orator who would impress us all with his eloquence. Instead he was a common mountain boy from the hills of Virginia. He used a lot of illustrations dealing with farming, and I could relate to that. One thing he said I'll never forget.

"A lot of us are like an old mule on the side of a mountain. The farmer wants to plow his field and tries to make the mule go in the right direction, but that stubborn ol' animal just is determined to go his own way. Many people are that way. God is trying to turn us around and head us in the right path, but we are so stubborn we just keep on going our own way."

That really struck me. I had made a lot of plans for my life, but God had no part in them.

That summer I was back on the farm, working and sweating and growing crops as usual. But something was different. I felt restless. I missed being with the group at school. I'd go to church, but something was lacking there. It was as if those folks were just playing church. The feeling of excitement and commitment I had observed in my friends at K State was lacking.

When I returned to the campus in the fall, I got another room in the same house. I was lying in my bunk one night thinking about the difference in these friends. They seemed to have a spiritual dimension in their lives that I lacked. They had really had an encounter with the living God. All the Scriptures I'd been hearing about how Christ had died for my sins and how I needed to repent and turn to Him in faith came back to me.

I thought and thought, until finally I just had to pray. "Lord, I've been just like that old mule Bob Finley told about. I've been going my own way, doing what I've wanted, never considering Your plans for my life. Please forgive me of my sins and give me this new life in Christ I've seen in others. I don't want to be four-F in Your kingdom."

I told my dad about the spiritual experience I had had and how my life had been changed. He snorted and replied, "Well, I've gone to church all my life, but I don't think you should be a fanatic about religion."

Mom was different. She seemed genuinely thrilled, and I discovered we spoke the same language. Talking with her made me remember the many times she had made baskets of butter, milk, cottage cheese, eggs, and other foodstuffs and taken them to the Gospel Missionary Union in the slums of Kansas City. Her interest in mission outreach suggested to me that she had a commitment to Christ that was more than just "religion."

As Inter-Varsity grew stronger on the K State campus, I became more and more involved. We formed a gospel team that sang and gave testimonies anywhere we had an opportunity. Whenever we were anywhere near our farm I'd take my friends by to meet my folks and treat them to samples of my mother's cooking. Dad seemed impressed with my friends. We were living good clean lives, and he appreciated that, although he couldn't quite tie the whole life-style together.

When word circulated that IV was going to sponsor a missionary conference in Urbana just after Christmas 1948, K State's whole chapter wanted to attend. I asked Dad for permission to drive our new Chevrolet coupe the 600 miles to the conference, and he agreed.

Our caravan of six or eight cars drove down old Highway 24 all night, but with six of us stuffed into my little two-seater, we didn't mind. We sang at the top of our lungs as we crossed the Mississippi at Quincy and drove across Illinois through the heart of all the little towns along the way.

We arrived in Champaign and became a part of more than 1,000 students milling around, inspecting the booths that had been set up by dozens of mission organizations. The booths were manned by missionaries from all over the world, and every one of them needed help.

There had been challenges about mission service at the newly formed College Baptist Church adjoining the Kansas State campus, but I had never made a serious commitment to leave our farm and serve the Lord in a foreign country. I knew how much it would hurt my dad to have his dream of a family farm vanish. At the same time I felt that since the Lord loved me enough to give His life for me, I couldn't pay for that, but at least I could show my appreciation by being willing to serve wherever He wanted me.

At the final service on New Year's Eve, a challenge was presented and "Purpose Cards" handed out. I checked the blank stating I purposed to be obedient to go to the mission field, *if* the Lord should lead me. The service closed with a Communion service at midnight. Starting the new year sharing Communion with so many dedicated young people was a tremendous blessing.

I didn't know it at the time, but in that crowd, sharing the same blessing, was a very special girl who would also change my life, a girl named Marilee.

It was a cold, rainy, miserable Saturday night in February when a buddy of mine, Loren Scott, and I drove the 100-plus miles from Kansas State to Kansas City for a Youth For Christ rally. We had just entered the vestibule of the old Grand Avenue Methodist Temple on Ninth Street when a mutual friend, Gloria Holton, called out to us.

Gloria was a nursing student at Kansas City's General Hospital, and Scotty and I were both at the stage of life where we were asking God to provide us with life partners. She was a cute little blonde, so we both responded with a big "hello." She came over with a friend in tow. The friend was a tall girl who wore no makeup, had her hair in braids wrapped around her head, and wore a very subdued gray dress with buttons down the front. My first impression was, "Boy, she must really be spiritual!"

We all got to talking, and it was natural that the four of us proceeded to the balcony to sit together. Since Scotty was more aggressive than I, he took Gloria's arm and led her up the stairs. So I was stuck with the stranger, Marilee Robison.

As soon as we slid into our pew Marilee and I discovered there was a nail sticking up between us. "Boy, these YFC folks are going to make certain we don't sit too close, aren't they?" she quipped.

"They don't seem to be taking any chances," I agreed.

She gave me a big grin and let out a delightful laugh. We continued teasing about avoiding the nail, and I decided, "Well, at least she has a good sense of humor."

We stood to sing, and I couldn't help but notice her rich, well-trained voice. When the song was finished, she complimented me on my voice. "Well, I do sing in a double male quartet," I replied immodestly. "We're going to be singing here at the YFC rally in about six or eight weeks. I have to lock in the date with the director, Al Metzker, tonight. You'll have to come hear us."

"I just might do that." She smiled as she slid back into the pew, avoiding the nail. Just then a button popped off the front of her dress! I guess I should have pretended I hadn't noticed, but I couldn't help but laugh. She looked so embarrassed. She took my kidding good-naturedly, and I began to hope she really would come to hear me sing.

The night of the big performance our octet milled around the front before the services. My mother, who was always interested in our doings, was there to hear us. I looked up, and there was Marilee, wearing a lovely blue dress with puffy sleeves. She'd had her hair cut, and though she didn't look as "spiritual" as at our first meeting, she sure looked good to me.

I took Mother over and introduced them. They looked each other over pretty much, talked a few minutes, and seemed to form a mutual admiration society. Knowing my mother approved was all I needed. I decided that as soon as school was out I was going to have to start making a number of trips into Kansas City.

First chance I had I gave her a call. "How about going out to eat tonight?" I asked presumptuously. It had been six weeks since I'd seen her, but I figured she should have known I was going to call.

"Oh, I already have plans. Today is payday for the student nurses, so a bunch of us are going to celebrate having five dollars by going out to eat fried chicken."

I've never been one to take a "no" easily, so I said, "Well, let me take all of you." I ended up taking five student nurses out to dinner— and all they did was talk nursing. It wasn't the most exciting evening I'd ever had, and I had to pay the check for the whole gang.

By this time I was determined to get better acquainted, so I gave her another call a few nights later. "How about going to Union Station to pass out gospel tracts?" I asked. There was a long pause at the other end of the line. "Pass out tracts?" she repeated. Another pause. "Well, I guess so."

Union Station is just down the bottom of the hill from General

Hospital. Hundreds of people were busily scurrying from one train to another. I read from the Bible, and we had prayer. Then we went in, and I handed her a bunch of tracts and said, "OK, you go down this side, and I'll go down the other."

She hesitated, shook her head, and very timidly explained, "I've never done anything like this before. What do I do?"

"Oh, just smile and hand them to people. They'll take them."

"All right."

I watched her out of the corner of my eye while she gave it a good ol' college try. People responded to her well, and she warmed up to the task. Before long the two of us had covered the whole station. Then we went out to eat.

At last I had her alone, and we had a chance to talk. "The night I met you I had just come off duty when Gloria insisted I go to YFC with her," she explained. "There was no time to wash my hair or put on makeup. That's why I looked so dowdy." She went on to tell me that even though she had been brought up in a very strict Christian home, she had rebelled in her teens and become quite worldly for a while.

"It's only this past year that I've come back to the Lord," she continued. "Then I attended the Urbana Conference, and on New Year's Eve I signed a purpose card saying I'd be willing to be a missionary."

"You were at Urbana? So was I! I did the same thing. Just think, we've taken Communion together."

For some reason that seemed very significant to both of us.

On our next date I took Marilee to a rescue mission. We both gave impromptu testimonies, and when they asked, we sang an unrehearsed duet. I sang the melody and she harmonized for our first performance of "Nothing but the Blood." I figured it was time to take her to meet my family.

When we arrived at the farm my mother made a big deal out of the pink, fluffy dress Marilee was wearing. "I made it myself," she commented, and that made points with Mother, because she was quite a seamstress herself. My father wasn't much interested in "pink eyelette pique" so, as usual, he didn't say much.

After we sat down to eat I realized I had failed to mention to Marilee my family's custom of eating in silence. She chattered on gaily all by herself. Her monologue was quite enchanting, I thought, and she soon had us all laughing, but I wondered how my dad would react to this. I shouldn't have worried. After the meal we took Marilee out to inspect the stock, and she made over Dad's horses so much that he seemed very pleased with her.

"She seems like a good, strong, jolly girl," he declared when we were alone. "Probably make a good farmer's wife."

By fall it was an accepted thing that we were going to get married and go to the mission field together. When we discovered both our parents had been married on December 23, we made plans to do the same. A few weeks before the wedding I realized I had never really proposed. I have this habit of expecting people to know what I'm thinking, and I figured she should know I loved her and wanted her to be my wife. After all, we were already making wedding plans.

I'd always thought my dad was a man of few words but hadn't noticed the trait in myself. I felt confident the Lord had provided the wife I needed, but just to please her, one night I pulled her to me and whispered, "Marilee, I love you. Will you marry me?" Just as I had expected she went all fluttery and feminine on me. But I liked it.

All the newlyweds on campus were on short rations, so Marilee and I didn't feel we were unusual trying to live on love. We tried not to make undue calls on the family account. A big night out for us in those days was a trip to the little Army surplus trailer Richard Spare and his bride, Neva Jean, were renting, where the four of us would share a tea bag. There is something about passing a limp tea bag from one hot cup of water to another that brings people together, and a bond was created between the four of us that has endured over the years.

Because of the years of hard labor I'd put in on the family farm, I felt fully justified in drawing money from the joint account, and as long as I was at Kansas State all the family seemed to approve. But when Marilee and I decided to act on our conviction that the Lord was leading us to the mission field by enrolling at Bob Jones University for Bible training, my mother took me aside.

"Son, I just don't know how you will be able to continue to draw from the family account while you are away at school this time, with the way your father feels about it."

Dad had made it quite clear that he felt my responsibility was to stay on the farm and provide for my wife and expected child. He didn't understand why we should consider it important to go to some foreign field and share Christ with others who had never heard.

"Well, Mom," I responded, clearing my throat, "I'm willing to go

to school on faith. We'll need enough money to get us to South
Carolina, but once we arrive, I'll write no more checks on the family
account."

Marilee and I discussed it later, and we agreed that if we were
going to live by faith on the mission field, we might as well consider
this part of our training. It was tough, though, because I'd worked
on the farm all summer and had nothing saved for the coming school
year.

Marilee's folks, Lee and Mary Robison, disproved every negative
story I'd ever heard about in-laws. They were just great. They encouraged us in our determination to serve the Lord and backed us
in every way possible. "The Lord will provide for you," they assured
us.

He provided for us, all right—He provided jobs so that I could
work our way through school. There were times we were on short
rations, but we never starved. I remember the time the car ran out
of gas on the way to work, and I let it roll as far as it would go. I
got out and hoofed it the rest of the way, got paid that night, bought
some gas, and returned home. Our budget was tight, but our faith
was strengthened as we squeaked by financially.

Our biggest blessing during our days at Bob Jones arrived on
November 11, 1950. The night Marilee went into labor I ran all the
stoplights on the way to the hospital. I was hoping to be stopped by
the police, so they could offer to escort us, but naturally none spotted
us. Our beautiful little daughter, Mary Beth, arrived the next morning, and I'll never forget the thrill of seeing her for the first time. It
was love at first sight.

Our second year at BJ our biggest concern was, "What mission
should we go with?" There were so many needs around the world,
but we wanted to find just the right place where our abilities could
best be used. Marilee came dashing in from a missions class one day
excitedly proclaiming, "I think I've found just the spot for us. A Mr.
Etter spoke to our class today, and their work in the Philippines
meets all three of our priorities. They want someone to work with
the children of lepers, do evangelistic work, and start an agricultural
project."

That was the beginning of our association with the International
Christian Leprosy Mission (ICLM). Before graduation it was made
official by ICLM, and we were ready to start deputation. We bought
an RCA 16-mm sound projector at a reduced price and the latest

BJU gospel film entitled *You Can't Win*. While we were speaking to raise support, we also wanted to present an evangelistic message.

We were manning a booth for the mission at the Winona Lake Bible Conference that summer when word came that my mother had had a stroke. We got home just in time to tell her good-bye. Returning to the farm from the hospital, I walked into the kitchen and stood staring at the sink where Mother had spent so much of her life. For the first time I really looked at the plaque hanging above her work spot. It read: Only One Life, 'Twill Soon Be Past, Only What's Done for Christ Will Last. Those words became very precious to me, for they summed up her philosophy of life.

Dad seemed adrift without her. The house was so empty. When our second daughter was born we named her Joy Phon, to keep alive my mother's middle name. That might have been the reason Dad formed a special attachment to that grandchild. With mother gone he seemed to resent even more the fact that we were going halfway around the world to serve people we'd never met instead of staying home where we were needed by the family.

"A man is supposed to provide for his family," he insisted. "How are you going to do that in a strange place like that? You don't know if they'll be safe. They'll have no security."

All his arguments were very logical. My only response was, "We'll just depend on the Lord, Dad. He will take care of us, provide for us, be our security." I didn't mention how slowly our support money was coming in.

"It looks as if our main support is going to be through friends in Inter-Varsity and members of the College Baptist Church," I told Marilee as the time for our departure grew near.

"Well, that's not bad," she replied. "We know those people really care about us, and they will not only be faithful in supporting us with their money, but they'll pray too."

"I know that's important, but we still lack five hundred dollars to buy the car the mission says we need. None of them have that kind of money. I don't know how the Lord is going to supply it."

A check for $250 came in from a Texas couple we didn't even know. I wrote them a thank-you note telling how they were half the answer to a prayer. A special delivery letter came back from them with a check for $256 more. "Forgive us for our unbelief," they wrote. "God told us to send $500, but we couldn't believe Him and sent only half. Here's the rest of the answer to your prayers. If we

had believed God, you would have had it the first time. The six
dollars is the first of the support money we will be sending you
monthly."

That really bolstered our faith. With great joy we picked out a new
bronze-colored Chevrolet Handiman station wagon. We had Acts
16:31, "Believe on the Lord Jesus Christ, and thou shalt be saved,"
painted on the back in fluorescent letters. Then we stuffed it and a
trailer with our equipment and all our belongings and prepared to
head for Seattle.

I'll never forget leaving my dad. He stood on the porch and
watched as Marilee and his two precious little granddaughters got
into the car. He looked so wretched, for he knew this was the end
of his lifelong dream of having a family farm. If only Mother had
been there with him. He looked so alone. I put my arms around him
and told him I loved him. He just shook his head and said, "I'll never
understand you taking your family over there. We ought to have a
funeral for you."

2

Real Missionaries?

The Evangel Baptist Church in Portland, Oregon, held a commissioning service for us during their annual missionary conference before we sailed for the Philippines. The pastor, Dr. David Laurie, was on the board of the International Christian Leprosy Mission. Listening to his Scottish burr resound in the huge building, I kept thinking about some advice Dr. Bob Jones, Sr., had written me: "There are too many armchair missionaries in Manila already. You get out and start winning souls." That was my heart's desire and my vow during our commissioning. I wanted to be a *real* missionary.

While presenting Marilee and me with beautiful new Bibles, Dr. Laurie made a statement that spoke to my heart. "Remember," he advised, "your stops as well as your steps are ordered by God."

During the reception that followed we met a young woman who was also going to the Philippines. Vivian Forsberg was going as a Bible translator under Wycliffe. "Who knows, we may meet again," she prophesied. She seemed as excited about beginning her first term as we were. But afterward I confessed to Marilee, "I still don't feel like a missionary."

She giggled. "What does a missionary feel like?"

"I'm not sure," I admitted. "Surely we'll find out after we get to Manila."

The first days of the voyage across the rolling Pacific, all I felt was seasick. I was really miserable during the days of rough seas. After we reached the southern waters and angled off toward Hawaii it became quite pleasant. There were only twelve passengers on the Dutch freighter, the SS *Rempang,*and we were allowed the run of the ship. We walked the decks, looked around in the engine room, and played endless games of ping pong. I beat Marilee all the way across the Pacific.

I even got permission to show the film *You Can't Win.*Since entertainment on board was very limited, everyone turned out. I found it exhilarating to have an opportunity to give witness for the Lord even while enroute to the field. That kind of made up for missing our fourth anniversary. We went to bed on December 22, crossed the international date line during the night, and awoke on December 24.

We had a Christmas party the next day, and the crew tried to make everything nice for us, but everyone was getting anxious to arrive by that time. On the last day of 1953 we saw land for the first time in over two weeks. As we sailed between some of the small Visyan Islands of the Philippines we saw our first palm and coconut trees swaying in the warm breezes. It was very exotic and exciting.

On New Year's Day as the new president, Ramon Magsaysay, was being inaugurated, we sailed into Manila Bay. Our delight turned to pathos as we viewed the sunken hulls of innumerable ships. The bay was full of old wrecks from the war. Masts were sticking out here and there, and we could see parts of hulls as we sailed directly over some of the sunken decks. By the time someone pointed out the infamous island of Corregidor I felt quite choked up. I'd missed the war, but I felt deep in my soul that I would do everything I could to see that those men had not died in vain. I realized that apart from them I would not be coming to the Philippines as a missionary.

As we docked we spotted a crowd of fellow missionaries and national Christians awaiting our arrival. Their warm reception made us feel quite humble. That night there was a combination New Year's and welcoming party attended by nearly all the fifty or so missionaries in Manila. I was particularly impressed by Cyril Brooks, senior missionary with Christian Missions in Many Lands, who had been in the Philippines since 1922. Mr. Brooks told us some of his family's experiences during the war.

"We were placed under house arrest," the tall, slim, dignified-looking gentleman told me. "For three and one half years we got no mail. That meant our income was gone. Our family—my wife, Anna, and Lynn, Ken, Rose, and myself—was given one red arm band with Japanese characters on it. To leave the house, we had to wear the arm band, which identified us as enemy aliens. I'm sure they didn't mean this for good, but it turned out that way, because the people understood our predicament. When we went to market, we'd never have to bargain. They would give us their very lowest price. Often they'd give us extra. We even had complete strangers come up to us and press money into our hands. The Filipinos really demonstrated their graciousness to us.

"We tried to carry on our mission work as best we could. We held services in the Tagalog language at the San Juan Gospel Hall," he explained. "The last eight months, when the war was going badly for the Japanese, they put us into an internment camp. Things were really bad there. We had to eat banana tree leaves—and then the roots. Some people even ate slugs.

"Then on February 21, 1945, the American paratroopers arrived at 7:00 A.M.—just two hours before the Japanese intended to massacre the twenty-one hundred people in that camp. That was a great day." He stopped his narrative long enough to take out a handkerchief and blow loudly. "We really looked pitiful. I was down to a hundred five pounds, my wife had beriberi and weighed only eighty-five pounds, but we were free!"

As Mr. Brooks continued giving more details of their experiences, I thought, *Wow, these people are* real *missionaries!*

"You'll find that driving here in Manila is very scriptural," Howard Eppler explained as we drove into the downtown section on our way to the post office. I observed the madcap interweaving of cars, jeepneys, trucks, and buses as they sped along MacArthur Boulevard and shot him a quizzical look. "Every man does that which is right in his own eyes," he explained.

I listened intently as Howard, the senior missionary for ICLM, gave me a crash course in Philippine red tape. I wondered how I'd ever learn my way back to the house, let alone which buildings held which offices and whom to see where. "The one good thing about having to come to the post office daily is that all the other missionaries do the same thing, so that gives you an opportunity to visit a bit and keep up with what is going on."

That was encouraging, for Marilee and I had been a bit dismayed when we learned the Epplers were planning to return to the States for furlough in just six weeks. If they weren't going to be available, at least I'd be able to ask questions of other, more seasoned missionaries. The idea of being left on our own so soon was a bit unsettling, but our desire above all else was to be a good witness for the Lord to our new Filipino friends.

Everything was interesting and exciting. The smiling faces along the crowded streets indicated that the people still appreciated Americans for having liberated them nearly a decade before. "Hi, Joe!" I was told over and over, often hearing the call from men squatting flat-footed along the busy thoroughfares.

We moved into the home the Epplers had been renting in the San Juan district of Manila, and as we emptied our boxes, they filled them with their belongings. I was quite pleased with my packing job. Since we were charged freight by the cubic foot, I'd squeezed everything into the smallest space possible. I even packed groceries in the bed springs. After the seventeen days enroute, we were relieved to find that the rat-proof, moisture-proof containers had done their job well. Everything was intact.

We found adjusting to living in a foreign country much easier than we had anticipated. Most Filipinos speak some English, so the language barrier was not traumatic. We had a comfortable home, and the biggest adjustment was getting used to having house girls to help with the work and being called "ma'am" and "sir."

The food was good and plentiful. We learned to eat lots of rice, but beef, pork, fish, and fresh vegetables were also available. Marilee quickly learned to cook many Filipino delicacies, and I enjoyed them. The main problem with the food was the stuff we'd brought with us. In my zeal for packing tightly I hadn't considered the consequences of wrapping Bisquick and bars of Sweetheart soap together. For the longest time everything Marilee baked tasted like Sweetheart soap. We could hardly stomach it but couldn't afford to throw it away.

Mary Beth and Joy were the objects of a great deal of friendly curiosity. With their platinum blonde hair, white skin, and big blue eyes our little girls were the center of attention wherever we went. This proved to be a good icebreaker and helped us to be friendly with people, but the girls started acting quite shy and self-conscious, and we had to protect them from too much curiosity.

Before the Epplers set sail, Howard outlined my responsibilities. The mission had five small cottages, really bamboo shacks with nipa grass roofs, that were used as homes for the children of lepers. We were to visit them several times a week to deliver the food money to the housemothers and have prayer meeting with them. Once a week we were to hold Bible class in the Protestant chapel at the leprosarium. Once a month we were allowed to take the children to see their parents. This made a touching scene, for the children would squat on one side of the road while the patients remained on the other. They couldn't touch one another but seemed thrilled to see each other and be able to talk across the road.

There was also a Saturday night Bible class for service personnel held at Sangley Naval Base across Manila Bay. We were to study the Tagalog language and to look for land to begin an agricultural project to help the lepers who had been declared in remission, since they were not readily admitted back into the mainstream of life.

The mission had started a nursery for the babies of lepers to keep them from having bodily contact with their parents. For the most part the babies were being cared for by the genial Miss Gussie Thiessen, R.N., with help from Marilee. Gussie was a queen-sized Mennonite who believed stongly in the Protestant work ethic. Her biggest problem was a growing supply of babies in too-small quarters on the ground floor of our home. My main responsibility with the nursery was transporting sick babies back and forth to the Mary Johnson Hospital. Because most of the babies were premature, they had many physical problems.

The problem with this schedule was that I needed more work to do. I was used to long hours in the saddle and felt strongly that my primary purpose for being in the Philippines was evangelism. So I started looking for places to show *You Can't Win.*

At the Far East Broadcasting Company (FEBC) I met one of their radio preachers, Pastor Anacleto Lacanilao, who had the heart of an evangelist. Once he learned we had this film and the necessary equipment, he kept us busy day and night. He'd call up in the middle of the afternoon. "Oh, say. We will go tonight to Pampanga." I wouldn't know where Pampanga was, or how far, but I'd say "Sure."

He'd come over, we'd drop the tailgate on our station wagon, slide in our projector, screen, loud speakers, and generator, and off we'd go. When we arrived at whatever site he'd chosen we would string lights from tree to tree in the town plaza, set up the screen, slide the projector onto the tailgate, crank up the generator, and we were in business.

People came out by the hundreds. Sometimes we'd stop in towns that were just wide places in the road, and 300 to 500 people would turn out with no advance arrangements or announcements. I guess we were the best show in town. He'd get up and say, "This is Pastor Lacanilao from FEBC . . ." and the people would gather. We'd start showing the film, and then right in the middle he'd say, "Let's stop and preach." I'd cut the film off right in the middle, and he'd preach for an hour in the local dialect, and the people would stay because they wanted to see the rest of the film. After the movie he would give an invitation to accept Christ, and we would have decisions every time. Always. Then we'd give some Christian literature and invite them to listen to FEBC.

Because Anacleto could speak half a dozen different dialects, we went farther and farther into the hinterlands, and people would always gather. He always wore the traditional *barong tagalog*, the long-sleeved formal shirt with tucks and embroidery typical of the Philippines. Perhaps that is why they would listen so attentively to his eloquent presentation of the gospel.

Occasionally Marilee and the girls would come with us, but the little *monicas* ("dolls") were really a distraction. And although I'd become used to people feeling the hair on my arms and peering at my blue eyes, for a five-year-old and a two-year-old it was unnerving.

While Anacleto was keeping my evangelistic zeal whetted at night, the days were getting more and more busy. We'd found a large house for rent nearer the leprosarium. It was ideal for our purposes. It had fifteen rooms and four bathrooms, and the downstairs was completely separate from the upstairs living quarters. And it was less rent than we had been paying.

As Mr. DeGuzman, the landlord, showed us around the house he kept asking us questions. "How is it in America? Why would you leave America to come here? Why would you want to care for these babies?" We talked a long time about our mission, our work, why we had come. He was very curious about our "religious philosophy." After a long discussion he asked, "How can I be born again?"

We explained as clearly as we could and he decided, "I like your philosophy of life. What school did you attend? I want to send my son to America to that school." Not long after we moved in, his oldest son was off to Bob Jones, and he and his wife became members of the Bible study group we started in our new home.

With Gussie Thiessen living downstairs with the babies, and our family upstairs, we were very happy with the new arrangement. Then we heard of a rumor going around the neighborhood that "Mr. Barker has two wives." We did our best to dispel that notion. We wanted to be a witness to our neighbors. For that reason we'd invite them into our yard for showings of *You Can't Win*. The squatters living nearby would flock over as well as the landowners, but as soon as the lights came on after the showing they would all scatter.

While living in Balintuak we had a new addition to our family, a German shepherd puppy we named Dutchess. We invested the money in a thoroughbred because we wanted her to be a good watchdog, and we figured that having a female, we could get our investment back with interest when she produced pups. Mary Beth and Joy fell in love with her immediately, and the pup reciprocated so strongly I began to wonder if she'd make a watchdog or not.

We had had Dutchess only three or four months when she disappeared. I searched for her almost all night. It was quite frustrating, because I could hear her whining and barking, but I couldn't locate her. I figured someone had locked her up.

Then we faced a real spiritual crisis. Our little girls started praying every night for their puppy to come home. We tried to explain to them that someone had taken the dog and probably sold it, that it was impossible for her to come back to us. But they kept on praying. Weeks went by. Then months. Still they prayed earnestly for the return of their pet. How can you explain to a child that some things are just impossible? Marilee and I were both concerned because we didn't want them to lose their child's faith.

Six months after the dog had disappeared we heard a noise outside our front gate, and there was Dutchess! I could hardly believe my eyes. She was skinny and mangy looking, and her ears were beat up and sore, but there was no doubt it was Dutchess. I brought her in, and we tried to feed her, but she wouldn't eat. It was obvious she had been mistreated. She just kept whining and trying to go to the back of the house. Finally we let her, and she went straight into the girls' bedroom. What a joyous reunion! After she had seen the girls she came back into the kitchen and ate.

The neighbors had all heard about the missing pup, of course, and when she returned they all had to see her for themselves to believe she was really back. One of the DeGuzman boys, Bonier, looked at her with big round eyes and whispered, "She's a miracle dog!" And I guess she really was, for she taught me to never underestimate the faith of a child, and the Lord's graciousness in returning her was a witness to all our neighbors, a stronger, more impressive witness to them than anything I'd ever said or done. She was a demonstration that God does answer prayer.

"One thing I don't understand," I told Marilee late one night as I lay awake thinking. "I'm supposed to set up an agricultural rehabilitation program for the lepers and their families, but we have no land, no farm equipment, and no money. Does the mission expect me to perform miracles?"

"Well, we're supposed to be faith missionaries," she countered. "Maybe we're supposed to have faith to believe the Lord will supply all this for us. He did promise to supply all our needs."

"I know that," I mumbled. "Didn't I say just that in our last prayer letter? I just feel that some way I should be putting feet to our prayers. The perfect solution would be to have someone give us that seventy hectares of land right behind this house."

"Who owns it?"

"I don't know."

"Why don't you find out?"

That sounded reasonable, so the next day I started asking around. Everyone said there was some dispute about just who had legal right to the land. A Madam X claimed it was hers, but the government claimed it belonged to them. I ran everywhere trying to find someone who could give me some definite answers. I found the mysterious Madam X owned a large hotel in Manila, so I tried to see her. I went from one office to another in the governmental buildings and finally got as far as the executive secretary of the president. He suggested I go see the mayor of Caloocan, so I trotted down there.

"Well, you know, that land is conflicted," he informed me.

"Yes, I do know. But the land is just sitting there idle, and it could be used to help these lepers. And all the little, innocent children. We don't want to own the land, we just want permission from the government to use it. When the government needs the property, we'll move out."

After a lengthy discussion he smiled and said, "Well, you know I can't give you permission to use the land, but I'll not molest you if you occupy it."

So we became squatters. It was really quite an arrangement. We were using the land and didn't have to pay rent or taxes. As Americans this didn't seem quite right to us, but the Filipinos all seemed to think this was fine, since it was such an accepted practice in the country.

First we built a kind of bunkhouse with two stories, three rooms up and three rooms down, with money we scrounged from the food allotment. We wrote home about our need for seed, and people donated generously. Next we borrowed a carabao from one of the lepers and started plowing up an area for sweet corn.

Maybe I should explain a little about carabaos. Technically the carabao, or water buffalo, is a member of the bovine family, but it is the workhorse of the Philippines. They are extremely strong, but slow and drawn to any pool of water. The men hooked this one up to a single-handled wooden plow. It was interesting to watch them handle the animal with just the one rope that went through his nose. When they pulled on the rope, he went to the left; a tap would turn him right.

It was interesting but *slow*. After a couple of days of watching these men loaf around, resting as much as working, I figured I'd teach them how a farmer from Kansas works. I taught them all right and nearly killed the carabao. I forced him to go full speed for half a day, not knowing that these animals have no sweat glands and can't take the heat. They convinced me that the carabao must work at its own speed and cool off in some water every couple of hours. Thankfully, he survived, and I learned another lesson about living in the tropics.

The fresh, beautiful soil that had never been used for farming before was soon producing well. We had a ready market for the large, sweet ears of corn we were producing. Each family also had a garden of its own, but there was enough land available that we could also plant upland rice. There was no way we could plant anymore, though, with that unenergetic old carabao.

"What we really need now is a tractor with a plow and a disk," I told Marilee one day as she was changing diapers in the nursery.

"Well, the land has been supplied. Let's pray for the equipment."

"Yeah. It'll be interesting to see how the Lord meets this need, because it'll cost at least three thousand dollars, and you can't just borrow something like that."

That Saturday night Marilee, Gussie, and I took the naval launch over to the base for the Bible class. It was always fun to ride across Manila Bay as the moon rose above the water. We'd get to fellowship with Americans and have some real American ice cream at the snack shop before catching the last boat back to Manila.

During the class, I mentioned our need for farm equipment and asked for their prayers. After Bible study this tiny girl, a Navy nurse named Dottie, came up to us and asked, "Could you use a truck?"

We had been praying for a tractor, and we didn't have too much need for a truck, but I've always worked under the philosophy that if the Lord offers you something, take it. So I replied, "Yeah, we probably could. What condition is it in?"

"I'll have to check on that, but you see, I'm eligible to get surplus equipment, and I thought that way I could give a better gift than if I just gave you cash. This will have to be cleared with the Pentagon first, but that will probably just be a matter of red tape."

Later in the week we got a phone call from her. "We could have a tractor instead of a truck," she said. "Would you prefer that?"

"We could really use a small one for our gardens. Is it a small tractor?"

"Oh, yes. Just a small one."

We hustled over to the base the first chance we had to inspect this "small" tractor. It might have been considered small in the eyes of the Navy, but it was an old TD-9 International on tracks. The huge monstrosity had a bucket loader in front and had obviously been carried there and parked. It couldn't have got there under its own power. I looked at the thing and thought, *I'm supposed to plant gardens with that?* It wasn't even in running condition, but I didn't want to discourage Dottie, so I said, "Sure, we'll take it."

The officer helping her clear the gift with the Pentagon promised to deliver it to Manila for us. I didn't know where we could get tools or spare parts to make it operational, but I said, "OK, by the time you get permission from the Pentagon, I'll have a place to have it delivered."

An implement dealer was a member of Grace Church. I didn't know him well but figured I could ask him for advice. When I entered John Sycip's office at the National Merchandising Corporation he stood, extended his hand, and gave me a broad smile. The stocky Chinese fellow was so gracious you would have thought I was a long lost friend. I told him the whole story.

"So I was wondering if we could bring the TD-nine into your compound for repairs. That would give us a place to check it out to see if it is possible to fix it."

"Hm. I tell you what, Jerry," he replied thoughtfully. "I've been needing a tractor like that. Would you be willing to trade that one, as is, for a little Ford tractor in running condition, with a plow and a disk?"

"Would I? John, that's a gold mine!"

"Well, bring it on in, and we'll just trade you for it."

I was discovering that this business of trusting God was exciting. We still didn't have any money, but we had land and equipment, and, besides, this contact with John gave us the opportunity of getting to know the Sycip family. Over the years their friendship became much more valuable than the tractor.

"I have a need of my own," Marilee complained one morning as she was dressing.

"What's that?"

"Some maternity clothes," she wailed in a voice that said I should have noticed.

This time the Lord provided through Mrs. DeGuzman. She already had eight or nine children, so she was well supplied with maternity apparel. She must have picked out her very best clothes to share with Marilee, because my wife was quite pleased with them. "When the Lord supplies, He does it with class," Marilee proclaimed as she paraded around in her new duds.

I never was one to be impressed with clothes, but I surely was impressed with my son. John Lawrence Barker was born on January 16, 1956. He was little—only six and one half pounds, but healthy, and he had a receding hairline to match mine. Instead of being jealous of him, Joy soon became his playmate and Mary Beth his little mother.

That spring Marilee and I finally got to take a concentrated course in the Tagalog language at one of the universities in Manila. We really needed that. It was embarrassing for Mary Beth and Joy to be correcting us all the time. Someone was always saying, "Oh, your children know Tagalog better than you do."

Because of language study we decided not to have Vacation Bible School that year, but so many of the parents wanted us to that we again opened our home to fifty or more youngsters each day. With VBS, language studies, evangelistic meetings, and our regular duties, we were kept busy that year, yet there was something lacking. I couldn't quite put my finger on it, but in one of our nocturnal discussions Marilee and I discussed the future.

"We have so much to be thankful for," I realized. "The Lord has supplied our needs abundantly. The kids are all healthy, we found a school for Mary Beth, before long our home Bible study is going to be ready to form a church. There's plenty of work to keep me busy, yet I'm not satisfied. I'm not sure what it is."

"Well, I don't think the Lord meant just money when He promised to supply all our needs," Marilee mused.

"Oh, I agree with that," I replied. "Look at the way He supplied us with spiritual advisers when we needed them. I don't know how we would have accomplished anything these past years if it hadn't been for Ed and Helen Spahr from Grace Church and Cyril and Anna Brooks from San Juan Gospel Hall. They have become, in effect, our spiritual parents.

"Yes," I continued, "He does supply all kinds of needs. But I need a new challenge. Everything now seems to be going along fine. I just don't feel all that needed anymore. I really want to be on the cutting edge, where I can be the most useful for the Lord."

"So pray for a new challenge." Marilee yawned sleepily. "But that sounds rather dangerous to me. He just might answer."

"Why don't you go to Mindanao?" John Sycip asked nonchalantly. From everything I'd heard about Mindanao it was a wild and woolly land akin to the old Wild West in the States. The second largest and southernmost of the Philippine Islands, it had been populated by Moslem tribes along the coastlines and exotic tribal groups in the interior mountains until recent years. Because there was much open, highly cultivatable land that had been standing idle, the government had begun moving in settlers to homestead the land since the war. Many rebellious groups from northern Luzon and criminals from overpopulated jails had been sent down there where they would have a chance to begin life over. Even the idea of visiting the island would send most people in Manila into spasms of terror. Everyone had heard stories of beheadings from the huge bolo knives that were used instead of pistols, of revenge killings, and of vendettas that made life cheap down in the hinterlands of the uncivilized island.

"Well?" John insisted. "Why not? It's really a beautiful island and not as wild as the stories you hear. Most of all it is wide open for the gospel. Cotabato, the southern part of the island, is developing like wildfire. The opportunities are unlimited. It's a real challenge."

Challenge? He'd said the magic word. "You, uh, want me to go down with you on one of your trips?" I asked hesitantly. I knew John had business all over. He had been helping the government mechanize Cotabato by importing Massey-Harris tractors. They were made available to groups of farmers for very low down payments and no-interest loans. I could see how this would be a challenging place for a farmer but wasn't sure how it applied to me.

"I'll tell you what I've been thinking about," John continued. "Some Christian businessmen in a place called Kalawag noticed the New Testament I always carry in my shirt pocket, and they approached me with an opportunity. It seems there is a small high school that is about to fold from lack of finances, and they want me to take it over and run it as a Christian school."

"But I'm an agriculturalist," I protested, "not an educator."

"Yes, I realize that. But there is land available. Farmland that could be used to finance the school, while teaching the students modern methods of farming. The students could work to earn their tuition, and the profit could pay the teachers' salaries, but they need someone with know-how to run the program.

"There is all kinds of equipment available. The US government donated fifteen million dollars' worth of farm equipment, but there's no one who knows how to use it. Some of it is still in crates. There are huge combines just sitting there, going to waste. Some of the farmers have used tractors, and when they break down they just come in and get a new one. There are no spare parts, and no one who can repair the machines. It's really a sad thing, this whole province, just waiting for someone to come in and cultivate it.

"There are many missionaries in Manila," he insisted, "but I don't know of anyone else who would be as qualified as you to accept this challenge."

That word again. And somewhere in the back of my head I recalled advice given me by another respected Christian leader, "Don't be an armchair missionary." I sighed. "OK, I guess I could go down there for a visit and look around. I have had the feeling lately that I've been working myself out of a job. Also, the senior missionaries for our mission are due back soon. Maybe the Lord has a new field for me."

It was May of '57 when John and I boarded an old Convair two-engine plane for the three-hour trip to Mindanao. I thought that plane was bad until we reached Cagayan de Oro, where we boarded a battered DC-3 for the "milk run" across the island. We got the grand tour, landing on half a dozen grass runways before reaching a place called Banga Compound near the Banga River.

Nothing was there but the airstrip and the machinery depot John had told me about, and he hadn't exaggerated. There were rows and rows of tractors, plows, combines, corn pickers—everything you could possibly use on a farm. Just sitting there, rusting. We then took the new gravel road that had been cut across the island to nearby Kalawag, where we inspected the 200 hectares of land adjacent to the high school, plus another 400 that John had leased. Six hundred hectares—nearly 1500 acres of rich, virgin land that had never been plowed or cultivated. It was all I could do to keep from drooling.

The school was another matter. There were just three little nipa houses made of bamboo with grass roofs. A three-room "Classroom Building," a two-story "Economics Building" that was in such sad shape we weren't allowed to go upstairs, and the principal's house.

There was one room set aside to serve as the library. It contained a
scarred table, three chairs, and no books. To say it was a pitiful setup
would have been an understatement.

A hundred or so students milled around, eyeing us with great
curiosity. They were shy, but friendly. The majority of them looked
very underfed.

"But you have to realize the potential," John kept telling me.

I had to agree there was no place to go but up. Things couldn't
have been much worse.

John had business elsewhere, so he flew off and left me with his
local employee, Harry Summers, an ex-GI who was in charge of the
National Merchandising Corporation. I climbed into a jeep with
Harry, and we flew all over the southern end of Mindanao. He was
a wild driver, but he had a good relationship with the people in
Cotabato and knew his way around.

The verdant island seemed a veritable paradise. The mountain
ranges were climaxed by a towering volcano named Matutum. Amid
so much lush, tropical beauty, it was heartrending to see such pov-
erty. If only the people knew better methods of cultivating their land.

We inspected a mountain of lime, where John had purchased a
lime factory that was no longer operating. "The government started
this project," Harry explained, "but they couldn't convince the farmers that the lime would help them. You know anything about it?"

"Yeah." I chuckled. "It so happens that lime was one of my father's
earliest projects. Matter of fact, back in nineteen twenty-four he was
the first to use lime as a fertilizer in our county. He even won a first-
place trophy for the best demonstration of the use of lime in growing
legumes. He would really be impressed with this. In the States if you
get fifty or sixty percent lime, that's a good percentage, but this hill
must be ninety percent. It's almost pure lime. All you have to do is
crumble it and spread it. If we could just teach these farmers to
neutralize their soil with this, their increased yield would be fan-
tastic."

"But how do you get them to try it?" Harry asked.

"That might be quite a trick. I guess you would have to use it
yourself, and demonstrate what it can do, like my dad did in Kansas.
Then too, if you had agricultural classes in your schools you could
teach the students, and a new generation would come up understanding good soil preparation."

I scuffed around in the white, powdery stuff a few minutes, thinking about my dad. He hadn't answered one of our letters since we

had left him back on the farm. Maybe something like this lime project would help him understand the need for people with know-how to share what they have learned with others. I wished he could be with me to see the tremendous opportunity in this newly settled province.

At least I was able to share all I had seen with Marilee. "It was the most challenging four days of my life," I bubbled over when I returned to Manila. I went on and on about all the opportunities, then explained, "The thing that spoke to me most was being invited to preach at the little Christian and Missionary Alliance church near the school. The place was packed, probably because the students were curious about this blue-eyed American. They listened so attentively. When I gave the invitation, a number of decisions were made.

"After the crowd had filed out, I noticed a skinny little kid, sitting alone way at the back of the church. His body was shaking with muffled sobs. I went back and talked to him a while, and he said he wanted to accept Christ as his Savior."

I realized tears were streaming down my face as I told my wife about leading that lad to Christ, but she understood. "Just a scrawny, little sixteen-year-old lad," I blubbered. "And I know it wasn't just my sermon that reached him, because he told me he had been taking Bible class in the school, but it seemed that having William Layda come to Christ was like a stamp of approval by the Holy Spirit. God was gracious enough to use my words to touch his heart."

We didn't want to make any rash, emotional decision, because we realized how this would affect our family as well as our ministry, so we talked to every Christian Filipino and missionary we knew. The advice seemed unanimous. "Go." Still I had one hesitancy, which I shared with Pastor Ed Spahr.

"I'm just worried about becoming too involved in secular things," I explained to him. "I fear there is a danger of helping people without reaching them for Christ."

Ed stretched his long frame and leaned back in his chair pensively. "Jerry, we've found here at Grace Christian School that it is like having Sunday school all day long. A church reaches these children maybe two or three hours a week, but we have them all day, five days a week. Every teacher should be evangelizing. They should be teaching secular subjects in a Christian atmosphere."

That statement was kind of a clincher to my decision, yet I hadn't fully committed myself when we went into the mountains of Luzon to Bagio for camp. Ken Brooks, Cyril's son; Ray Kalback, who was with the Grace Christian High School; and I had started a summer camping program back in 1954, probably the first Christian camps in the Philippines. We felt they were quite successful, as we had an opportunity to work with the young people on a deeper level during the weeks of camp. That summer the Holy Spirit was dealing with my own heart, and it was there in the picturesque beauty of Bagio that I sat down on a rock and prayed: "Lord, I'm willing to go to Mindanao. If it is Your will, open the way and make it possible."

I felt Marilee should have input into this decision, because she would feel the brunt of any hardships as she raised our youngsters in rather primitive conditions, so John arranged for us to make a trip to Mindanao together in September. He supplied us with Gideon Bibles to be given to the teachers at Kalawag Institute and a New Testament for each of the students. I watched my wife's face as these were distributed and could tell she felt the pull to come and help these eager people.

"It won't be easy," she acknowledged as we talked over our decision on the way home. "I'll miss the big house in Manila with running water and electricity, but this is where we belong, Jerry. I just know it."

I gave her a big squeeze. "It'll be tough, but we'll be pioneering. We'll be real missionaries."

3
"We Can Do It!"

Before we left on furlough John Sycip gathered a group of missionaries, business people, and Christian workers in his Manila home. They enthusiastically agreed that the Mindanao project was an opportunity for a Christian witness that could not be passed up. I was particularly heartened by the Christian and Missionary Alliance (C&MA), the main organization working in Mindanao. They said, "Come help us!"

The committee agreed to form a board of Filipino leaders so this would be an indigenous work. While we were on furlough, they would work out details for incorporation as a nonprofit, charitable organization to engage in education, medicine, orphanages, agriculture, and anything else we found was needed, including a radio station to be affiliated with FEBC. All I had to do was go back to the States and recruit some educators to take over the school administration and as many teachers as possible. Swept along by the enthusiasm of the committee, I believed finding willing workers would be a cinch.

Returning to the States, I discovered how much I had missed my country. Every time I'd see Old Glory waving in the breeze I'd feel a big lump forming in my throat. Being reunited with friends and loved ones was, of course, the highlight of our return. Dad seemed impressed that we had all come home alive. His granddaughters were still healthy, and he even had a new grandson. When he heard me giving a report to our church about our years on the mission field and when everyone made a big deal of "his son the missionary," he warmed up to the idea even more.

For $75 a month we rented a little house in Lawrence that was near both our families and set off on a speaking tour. It was great having time with folks who had supported us, not just with money, but with their prayers. Their questions reflected their love and concern for the people we had writtten about in our prayer letters.

It was a joy to be with the Spares again. Richard and Neva Jean no longer had to share tea bags, but they were working hard at making their farm fruitful while raising a growing crop of kids. It was very evident that the name "Barker" was quite familiar to their youngsters, because when we first walked in the kids acted as if they were meeting mythical characters. They'd been praying for us all their lives, but seeing us in the flesh was another matter.

The year was a success for raising funds and equipment, but recruiting was another matter. Interviews with prospects would invariably go like this:

PROSPECT: "What mission board are you with?"

ME: "Well, we don't have a board in the States yet, but one has been incorporated in the country with the name Philippine Evangelical Enterprises, Incorporated. This is a national work. We are going to be support personnel, helping them to get established."

PROSPECT: "What denominational backing do you have?"

ME: "None."

PROSPECT: "What financial security can you offer my family?"

ME: "None. We're just trusting the Lord."

PROSPECT: "Are homes ready for the educators you recruit?"

ME: "Well, no. But we'll find some kind of accommodations."

PROSPECT: "Well, uh, we'll let you know."

ME: "But it's a tremendous opportunity. Mr Sycip, our director, has hired a young man, Bob Poudrier, to work for him part-time and for the mission part time. Bob and his bride, Marian, are living in Cotabato City, and they write such encouraging letters. They say enrollment in the school has already doubled, and hundreds of new settlers are moving into Cotabato Province every day."

That would invariably be the end of the contact. Looking back, I can understand their hesitation. Who wanted to work for a thing that didn't really exist yet? I realize now that Marilee and I were very young and naive and just dumb enough to trust the Lord to take care of us even though we didn't know what we were getting into.

Then word came from John Sycip that Philippine Evangelical Enterprises, Inc. (PEEI) had purchased a second, larger school in Marbel, about thirty-five miles from Kalawag.

"Our prayers have gotten crossed up someway," I told Marilee.

"What do you mean?"

"We've been praying for more workers. Instead the Lord has sent more work."

"You'll be living in Marbel," Bob Poudrier informed us when we reached Cotabato City, Mindanao.

"Well, we'd figured on staying in Kalawag, near the farm project," I explained.

"But there is no house there. Nothing. The director of the school in Marbel has moved out of his home, and it is waiting for you. It's a three-bedroom house, has water, probably the nicest in town. Also, Marbel has electricity, and since it is the town center of the larger area of Koronadal, shopping will be much better. There's really not much in Kalawag. About the only thing Kalawag has that Marbel hasn't is a Moslem student."

"How's that?"

"Well, I was checking out some of Mr. Sycip's land a few miles outside Cotabato City, and I saw this Moslem kid gathering coconuts, and I started talking to him. He told me he'd had to drop out of school because of finances. I asked him if he'd like to go to school at Kalawag if I arranged tuition, and he said he'd have to ask his parents' permission, and they said it was OK."

"They gave permission for him to go to a Christian school?"

"I'm not sure he mentioned that. But I really like Badawi, and he seems to be doing fine. He's very appreciative. You'll get to meet him when you're over visiting that school."

"Just how far apart are the two campuses?" I asked.

"About a two-hour drive. What kind of transportation do you have?"

"We have a brand new three-quarter-ton Chevrolet truck coming," I explained thankfully. "When we left Manila we sold our station wagon, then a friend practically gave us a car to use on furlough. We sold that and put the money and some donations into getting a good truck."

"Great!" Bob grinned. "It'll be put to good use here."

"What is the new school like?" I asked

"Well, it's a more established school. They already have a fine board of directors and really want it to be a Christian witness, but they've just not been able to make it financially. The students can't afford the tuition, so the directors are really behind on the teachers' salaries. They need the added income your farm project will bring in."

"That's my top priority," I declared.

"They have three and one half hectares of land," he continued, "and three reasonably good buildings. At least the floors aren't falling in like at Kalawag. There are about one hundred fifty students enrolled and a good faculty."

"Well, Marilee, it looks as if we'll be living in Marbel," I informed her. She was busy with the kids and merely shrugged. She was such a good sport.

"About the farm project, Jerry. Mr. Sycip has made available twenty repossessed tractors, so I've started some of the drivers plowing those fields."

"Oh, good. We've got to get that land ready to plant upland rice. Since it has never been farmed before we can plant that variety without worrying about its being taken over by weeds. I'm really going to push getting that land ready so we can have a cash crop as soon as possible."

"Don't guess we'll be here to see it," Bob said. "I was hired to be temporary field director until you arrived, so we'll be leaving soon."

I was sorry to hear that, for they seemed like a very personable young couple. We spent a few days with them to give our possessions a chance to catch up with us and be with friends on Christmas Day. Instead of a white Christmas, this one was very green. We spent the day on the beach and had a lovely family time together.

Our fun was overshadowed by an inevitable event. I had to return to Manila with Mary Beth to enroll her in school. Being separated from one's young children is the hardest thing any missionary has to face, but we felt we had to provide our children with the best education possible.

When I had had a part in the founding of Faith Academy for missionary children while we were in Manila, I hadn't thought our children would ever be boarding students. Yet we were both thankful that we knew the school and the teachers who would be responsible for our daughter. Since she had attended the school in first grade she wouldn't be with strangers.

Bob Poudrier took Marilee and Joy and John on to our new home in Marbel while Mary Beth and I stayed behind to catch our plane. A young Filipino pastor and his wife would be staying with Marilee to help her adjust.

I think leaving Mary Beth at Faith Academy was harder on me than it was for her. She seemed excited and happy to see her friends and teachers she had missed while on furlough. Maybe all third graders feel they are quite grown-up, but to me she was still my little girl.

I had all kinds of business to take care of while I was in Manila. It made me realize how important the years with the leprosy mission had been, for without that experience I'd have been defeated before we ever began. One bit of red tape I enjoyed was making arrangements for our dog, Dutchess, to be shipped to our new home. I knew how anxious the kids were to see her again.

When I arrived in Marbel, I discovered things weren't quite what I had expected. The "best house in town" turned out to be an oddly constructed wooden building surrounded by dust. An extremely large, smelly hog had encamped in a low spot directly in front of the front door. Obviously he felt he had squatter's rights and intended to stay, but I had other ideas about that.

The interior revealed the oddest floor plan I'd ever seen. A tiny little bedroom stuck out here, and another stuck over there, and a little cubicle upstairs that was unbearably hot. The stairs went up from the middle of the kitchen, which wasn't quite what we'd hoped. It had a dirt floor, a cement and hollow-block wood-burning stove with a leaky stove pipe going through the ceiling, and in the center of the room a little pitcher pump. The room was hot, filled with smoke, and a muddy puddle surrounded the pump.

"It, uh, doesn't look like much, does it?" I ventured.

"Doesn't look like much!" Marilee repeated, her voice a couple octaves higher than usual. "That isn't the worst of it. There were so many curious eyes peering at us last night I finally had Mariano nail the windows shut. Then there wasn't a breath of air.

"As for shopping, there are a couple of sari-sari stores, where all you hear is, 'Sorry, we're all out of that,' and 'Sorry, we don't carry the other.' Downtown Karonadal has a 'department store,' but it will never be any threat to Macy's. We'll have to drive four hours to Cotabato City to shop. And there's no electricity, so with no refrigeration I'll have to buy fresh foods every day."

"I thought Marbel had electricity?"

"It does. From six P.M. till ten P.M. Only the wires don't reach out this far."

"It'll be a little tough for a while, until we can clean and fix things up a bit, but we can do it. At least we have *tubig*," I consoled her, glancing at the pump.

"Water?" She snorted. "Try it."

She said it as if it were some kind of challenge, so I gave it all I had. Soon I heard a muffled, gurgling sound, and I had water. But with an added bonus: worms.

"We have to be willing to sacrifice," I explained to Marilee, "so we can be an example to the staff. I'll put in a new well so we have good, clean, drinkable water, and we will make the house presentable, but we don't want to be living above the people."

The pig "sacrificed" his home in front of the front door, and we made plans to build a fence around the house, since it was located on the campus. That way our kids would have a yard of their own, and we could turn Johnny loose without losing him. Also, I'd plant some grass to cut down on the dust problem. I made plans for a little playhouse for the kids, what the Filipinos called a *bahaybahay*, a "toy house."

All in all, I was quite pleased with the way my family was adjusting to our situation. When Joy received a letter from my dad I knew that was his way of saving face and still opening the lines of communication. We heard from him occasionally after that, and having his support meant a lot to me.

While the improvements to the house were being made, I was running back and forth to Kalawag trying to get the farm project going. It was quite a sight to see those tractors opening the land. The grass was as high as a two-story house and swallowed the machines as they attacked it. The equipment was in bad shape, and I spent days running around trying to get parts to keep the tractors running. This got me acquainted with the drivers, and I found they were fomenting rebellion.

"They haven't been paid," I explained to Marilee. "You can't blame them for being disgruntled. It seems there was a crop failure last year, so their salaries are in arrears as well as the teachers' at both schools. We've inherited a situation where we aren't starting with nothing, but in the hole."

"Couldn't John Sycip just pay them?" she asked naively.

"Oh, Marilee, John keeps all his capital working. I'll bet he doesn't have more than a hundred pesos in his bank account, even though he's always working in six-figure deals. We can't expect him to pull us out. Our only hope is that the Bible conference we have scheduled will result in a real revival that will help heal some of the bitterness."

John had planned this conference as an evangelistic outreach, since many of the workers we had inherited were not Christians. We registered over fifty participants, mostly teachers and farmworkers, everyone connected with PEEI in any way. All day Thursday we felt a deadness and bitterness in the meetings.

In the evening meeting, one of the leaders of the rebellion stood to his feet, right in the middle of the sermon. This young fellow was so strong he had been nicknamed "Carabao." "I didn't come here to hear the Bible," he shouted. "I came here to kill someone! We want our money! Americans have money. Chinese Filipinos have money. We want ours!"

Mr. Sycip had come down for the meetings, and he tried to explain to everyone that missionaries, whether they came from America or not, did not have money and that his money was all invested in these schools. "But we will pay you as soon as our first crop comes in. If we all work together, we can pull out of this financial difficulty."

John Sycip had been a faithful witness in all his dealings in Mindanao, and the people respected him for this. He never missed an opportunity to read the Bible with them and to share his faith, so when he said, "Don't worry about this financial shortage. Just trust the Lord. We will all live by faith," they listened. After he spoke it was evident there was a division among the crowd. Thankfully, the Christians were able to calm down the unbelievers.

The next morning we had a prayer meeting for the speakers and spiritual leaders among us. The Holy Spirit's presence was evidenced by the burden that fell upon us as we wept and confessed our sins. There was a new attitude as one of our national speakers spoke immediately afterward. His message was very short, but the meeting turned into a time of confession of sin and restored fellowship with God among the Christians. Many came forward to accept Christ as Savior.

Not only did we see more people converted than we had expected in the first year of our ministry, but we were all brought into close fellowship, and we became a missionary organization in the true meaning of the name. Because we had explained it was going to be necessary for everyone to share during our times of financial strain, an offering was taken. These people had so very little to give, yet they gave out of hearts of love for the Lord. I'm sure the offering was a "widow's mite" for many of them. Teachers gave their watches. One woman put her earrings in the offering. "We want to help," they all said.

This really humbled me. Here I had thought the Barkers were

going to teach these people how to sacrifice. Instead, we learned a lesson.

After the Bible conference it was thrilling to see the changed lives and the different attitude of the workers. All of the teachers were now born-again believers and demonstrated a burden to reach the students for Christ. At one chapel service at Kalawag thirty-six young people became Christians.

Many of the farm workers also accepted Christ as Savior. I wish I could say this included the ringleader, Carabao, but he was among those who left. This weeding out of the unbelievers was necessary for the onward program of the Philippine Evangelical Enterprises, but still it hurt to see men like him leave with such a bitter attitude.

There was opposition from a number of sources. The students at nearby Notre Dame school were instructed to avoid meeting or talking with us. We showed the film *You Can't Win* all around the area and were often distracted by the sound of stones being thrown at the church. One evening the stones rolling off the roof were particularly noisy, and no one was surprised when a window was broken. "It's sort of a Philippine custom," Zoilo Espa, the pastor of the local C&MA church explained. "They are showing their disapproval. If you reprimand a student, you might have a stone on your roof that night."

Pastor Espa was one of the men who had been instrumental in interesting PEEI in buying the school we renamed King's Institute. One of the pioneer pastors in the area, he earned my respect as I observed his diligence as a pastor. His church and the Southern Baptist church were the evangelical churches in Marbel where our family worshiped. Having them nearby was a real blessing to us.

Another blessing was finding a missionary children's school at Malaybalay, in Bukidnon, a northeastern province of Mindanao. This was in a higher altitude where the climate is quite pleasant, and somehow, even though Mary Beth was still away from home, it was comforting to at least have her on the same island we were. The exhausting six hours' drive was longer than the flight to Manila, but a lot less expensive.

After three months of continual toil, the 600 hectares of land were finally ready to plant. That might seem like a long time, but my father had taught me the importance of preparing the soil correctly. When the rich, virgin earth was all mellow, soft enough so you could take a stick and punch a hole in the ground and drop a seed, John

Sycip got a bank loan for rice seed. While the tractors were planting the seed I stood and watched, mentally calculating how many million pesos the crop would bring us. A sack of rice, about 120 pounds, was selling for six pesos, and the rate of exchange was two pesos to one dollar. The figures were astronomical, and I began envisioning the new buildings and equipment we'd be able to have after squaring up with the teachers and workers for their back salaries.

Planting upland rice is like sowing wheat in the States. You have a grain drill about ten feet wide, and it plants rows about six inches apart. Sixteen rows on the ten-foot drill. Since the whole process was mechanized, this was probably the most beautiful planting ever on the island of Mindanao, a real demonstration of how it should be done.

During this whole process I'd often take Johnny with me to the fields, as my father had done to me. He was an extremely energetic three-year-old and seemed to have an inborn love for the soil and the machines. I was particularly pleased with the way he took to the big, noisy machinery. Not a bit afraid. I felt certain this early interest would one day be translated into a desire to spend his life on a plow. There's a special feeling that comes from finding a kindred spirit in your own son.

The rice began to grow. I truly believe you could farm a hundred years and there would still be a thrill at the first sight of fresh green shoots coming out of the ground. I'd drive over every morning just to see how much it had grown during the night, and in that soil, with the warm, moist climate I could really tell the difference day by day.

Marilee and I were sitting out front of our house, trying to catch a cool breeze one evening, and I was telling her about how beautifully the crop was growing, when she exclaimed, "Look! There is fire on the mountains!"

At first I thought she was referring to the orange glow cast by the setting sun, but then I realized the mountains really were on fire. "That's the old slash/burn method of agriculture at work," I told her. "It's beautiful, but very destructive. The natives cut down the grass and trees, whatever, at the bottom of the mountain, let it dry, then set it afire. The heat creates an updraft that spreads the fire up the mountain, burning everything in front of it." The fires were growing up the mountainside as I was explaining the process.

"But why do they want to burn everything?"

"All that ash will make the soil fertile, and if the trees burn also there will be potash. They don't need to plow, because the newly burned soil will be soft, and there will be no weeds or grass. It's good farming for a year or so, but then the weeds begin to grow. After two or three years the soil becomes badly eroded since it isn't taken care of and they just abandon it. Move on."

"What about the land they leave?"

"Oh, it is useless. Not fit to farm for another twenty years or so."

"Oh! So if there was an endless supply of land, that method would be all right, but with a growing population—"

"Exactly. The government knows this and is trying to discourage slash/burn, but what can they do? They don't even know how many tribal groups live in those mountains, let alone what the population is, and with settlers moving in, taking more and more of the land, this situation can't go on indefinitely. We're going to have to teach them modern methods of agriculture, or they'll starve."

The next day I was over at Kalawag, checking out the young, tender rice plants. They were about a foot and a half out of the ground, just going beautifully. It was so encouraging. All these people who had sacrificed were going to be repaid and we'd have a financial cushion that would allow us to make plans for the future. Standing there on that bright, clear, sunny day I felt on top of the world, even if I was only six degrees from the equator. I looked off to my left toward the mountains and spotted a cloud. *Fine,* I thought, *rain is just what we need now.*

The cloud began growing ominously. As it neared the farm it became a huge, black swollen mass. The air around me became still. Not a blade of the new rice was moving. Then I became aware of a high pitched, whining sound. Although the sweat was still rolling down my back, a chill overtook me, for I realized this wasn't a rain cloud. It was locusts.

The swarm was so thick it shut out the sunlight as the brownish-looking insects blanketed the green field. Back in Kansas we would have called them grasshoppers, although I'm told these have shorter antennae. The workers and I just stood there, helplessly, and watched. This was one time I wasn't embarrassed by the tears running down my face, for I wasn't the only one crying. We had all been banking on this harvest. We had accounts running all over the province, because the people had confidence in us. After all, I was an American. I had a degree in agriculture. I was supposed to know everything.

Within an hour the field was denuded by the locusts, and they moved on to greener fields. Literally. Swarm after swarm of the flying insects came, eating everything green in their paths. For days. Weeks. Big clouds swirling over every bit of living vegetation. They would land in a field of corn, and within two or three hours it would just be a bare field with not a stalk of green remaining. They ate everything green in the province, even the leaves off the coconut trees. There wasn't a green tree, or even a green stalk of any kind, anywhere.

We did everything possible to fight them. We'd buy rice bran and mix it with poison. The newly hatched crawlers would eat it, and there would be yellow piles of dead locusts. But they would just keep flying in. The government tried spraying poison, but they had to stop because people were dying. With nothing left to eat, they were eating the locusts, and some people had eaten poisoned locusts.

You have to be pretty hungry to eat locusts, but the people were that desperate. Two men would take a bed sheet and hold it like a sail. Then they'd run into a swarm and catch the bugs. It would take only minutes to get two or three sacks full.

I've never been more discouraged in my life. How could the Lord allow this to happen? It wasn't fair. Why had He turned His back on us? I hated writing reports back to our supporters during this time, but I felt strongly that it would be less than honest to write glowing reports of the good things that happened on the field and to fail to mention the troubles. Besides, our personal support was down and though we weren't eating locusts, we were reduced to rice and canned sardines.

The teachers and workers were in much worse shape than we were, and yet I'd hear words of encouragement from them. Pete Cargas, our agriculture teacher over at Kalawag, always had a big smile for me. He was young, a fresh graduate from Southern Mindanao University in north Cotabato and had the enthusiasm typical of his age. He'd come to Kalawag as his first assignment a year before, had met the Bible teacher the Philippine Missionary Fellowship had loaned our school, and had promptly married her.

"Eating locusts is scriptural," he teased. "Didn't John the Baptist eat locusts?"

"If you cook them right they don't make bad *viyand*," Avelina, his wife, added. "You boil them in water, then put salt on them. They are crunchy and taste a little like dried fish."

I just shook my head. *Viyand* is what Filipinos call whatever they eat with the rice they have three times a day. Sometimes they have

fish for *viyand,* or pork, or just vegetables. If someone was really
poor they would say, "Those people have only salt for *viyand.*" That
was bad enough; but locusts?

"Besides," Avelina continued, "the Lord is blessing in other ways.
Badawi has made a profession of faith. Our first Moslem convert."

That news and their attitude meant a lot to me. I returned to
King's Institute and began talking with the registrar, Mateo Llobrera.
He was a tall, scholarly man who also taught Spanish. He and his
wife, who was also a teacher, had five young children to feed. "Things
are hard," he acknowledged. "The students aren't even able to afford
their tuition of thirty dollars per year, and many are behind in
paying."

"How is your family making it?" I asked.

"Things are difficult at home also," he admitted, "but we know
the Lord will provide. Remember, we were here during the war. We
ate roots then to stay alive. We can do it again if necessary."

As much as I hated to do it, I went to check on Tatang Bajo, one
of the lepers we had met in Manila. Since his disease had been
arrested, I had invited the diminuitive man to come down to the
"promised land." Now I didn't know if he had enough to eat. *Tatang*
is a Tagalog term of respect which literally means "Daddy." He was
older than I, but that wasn't why I, too, called him that. He was a
fine and a dependable worker despite his disfigurement from leprosy.

"I guess it will be a while longer before I can earn enough to bring
my family down," he told me. "Right now, I am thankful they are
still in Manila where there is food to eat."

I found it touching that he could find anything to be thankful for,
and it made me question all the more just why the Lord would let
people like these suffer.

"I've been thinking about it, too," Marilee confessed at the dinner
table. "I've decided that maybe this is one of those 'stops' Dr. Laurie
told us about during our commissioning service."

"Oh, yeah. He said that a man's stops are ordered by the Lord as
well as his steps. I know in my heart that that is true, but it's still
hard to understand."

"But don't you see, Jerry, we came down here all full of ourselves.
We were going to do it all, and now we've been reminded that we
are nothing apart from the Lord."

The wisdom of her words struck me immediately. "You're right,"
I admitted. "We were going to demonstrate the power of good old

Yankee know-how. Show them the 'Can Do' spirit. With John Sycip's financial backing we thought we were invincible, but now the Lord has demonstrated His mighty power and how helpless we are apart from His blessing. I guess this is a lesson every Christian has to learn at least once in a lifetime. Whenever we get to feeling too independent, all He has to do is to send a few 'locusts' into our lives."

4

The Barker Hotel

The business of PEEI was carried on in a rather unorthodox manner. I'd get a wire from John Sycip, the president of the organization, saying he would be at the airport at such and such a time. Then the field director—that's me—would meet his plane. In the fifteen or twenty minutes his plane was on the ground, we'd transact all our business, and he would deliver letters and packages, then fly off.

Occasionally he'd call out as he was leaving, "I'll be back day after tomorrow at the same time, and I'll spend the night with you."

"We'll look forward to it," I'd call back, and mean it. John was such a jolly sort of fellow that everyone enjoyed having him around. Though he was rich in acquisitions he always had time to listen to anyone's problems or needs. His generosity extended not only to money, but time and consideration as well. If Marilee would mention, "My, it's been a long time since we've had hot dogs," the next plane from Manila would bring a package containing hot dogs. Or vitamins. Or medicine. Anything. He was just a kind, considerate man.

"I'll have to see if I can find some durian," Marilee would invariably respond when I'd tell her John was coming to spend the night, for she knew how he loved the luscious, tropical fruit with a smell that made Limberger cheese seem fragrant. She'd prepare a hot curry for dinner, another of his favorites, then for breakfast there would be homemade cinnamon rolls, fresh from the oven.

Whenever we were in Manila, our attempts at hospitality would be outdone by John and his gracious wife, Naty. Naty was a lovely

Filipina lady who never let caring for six children keep her from opening her home to anyone needing a night's lodging. No matter how inconvenient it might be, she made visitors feel like honored guests.

Our little house on the King's Institute campus was almost as busy—out of necessity. There just wasn't anyplace else for people to stay in Marbel. We never had less than seven for breakfast, and often seventeen or eighteen for dinner. "I sometimes feel as if I'm running a guest house," Marilee grumbled one evening.

"But isn't 'hospitality' one of the gifts of the Spirit?" I reminded her.

"I know, and I wouldn't mind so much if I had better facilities and more food to share."

"It is rather amazing how many people we pack into this little house some nights," I had to agree. "Maybe we should give you the title 'Official Hostess of PEEI.'"

As if being wife, mother, hostess, and teaching a couple of classes of English weren't enough for her, she added another title soon after. John was sitting at our dining table one evening when he suggested, "Why don't you start a cannery? Marilee, you taught the lepers how to can—you could do the same thing here. You'd be teaching these people a new method of food preservation, and the income from the cannery, with the money earned from putting our combines out in custom service, would help us pay the teachers something."

"That's a great idea!" Marilee exploded enthusiastically. "We could let some of the students work off their tuition, so our labor costs would be minimal. We'd have to start on a small scale, but a cannery just might grow into a really productive project."

My wife sometimes lets her enthusiasm run away with her. I had to wonder if she knew how much work she was letting herself in for, but John came up with the necessary equipment. We turned one of the older buildings with a dirt floor into a canning factory, and each evening we would can any corn we'd been able to buy.

Marilee was the manager, we had two or three employed people to act as supervisors, and twenty-five or thirty students at a time would line up for the assembly-line production. First they would shuck the corn, clean it, and scrape it off the cob. The more dependable workers cooked and ladled the corn into cans. We kept four tin-can sealers, old crank-type hand machines, going. The big bottleneck to the operation was the old kerosene burners underneath the sterilizers. They were so slow!

The students would work until eleven or twelve o'clock at night, then we'd leave the staff workers to finish the cooking process, and we'd go to bed. As the cans cooked, the ends would puff up, and you'd know you had a good seal. Then as they began to cool, the ends would snap back in, so all night long we could hear them popping. It was an annoying, yet comforting sound.

The "King's Quality" creamed sweet corn made quite a hit in Manila, and we had a ready market. We were limited by the amount of corn we could buy, since the locust infestation was followed by an invasion of rats. The students were allowed to work until they had paid off their tuition, and then they had to let others have a turn. Any kids who so desperately wanted to learn had to be good investments for the future.

One skinny little girl, about fifteen or sixteen, not only worked in the cannery at night, but would come early in the mornings to sweep out the "Barker Hotel" before going to class. "Mags, how do you keep up with your studies when you work so hard?" I asked the youngster, whose name was really Magdalena Maglunob, but like all Filipinos had a nickname.

"Well, sir, I come from a very poor family with eight children," she responded. "We are farmers, and we have to go to the field and weed the corn and the rice. It is so hot! A hard job! And very itchy. Every time I was in the fields I would always think, 'If I don't study I will grow old this way. There is no more hope to be improved.'

"That is why I didn't get married. Most of the girls in the elementary school where I was, they got married. I said, 'No.' They get married and have plenty children and their lives will be very hard. But people who go out to other places to study, they come back and they look so neat. So I think, perhaps I could also get an education, and I could speak English, and I could read books, and my life will not be so hard."

"Couldn't your family help you at all?" I asked.

"Oh, sir, they are so poor they have to divide eggs," she explained. "My father inspired me, anyway. He said he would sell the cow so I could go to school. I couldn't let them sell their cow for me, so I work hard to earn my tuition. Someday I will be a teacher. The Lord will help me."

There was no lack of young people who wanted to study. Our greatest need was for qualified teachers. But how do you recruit more teachers when you can't pay the ones you have? We were in the middle of a missionary conference at the school when the Lord provided a couple of gems. During one of the services Romeo and Trifina Mojica walked in. I first met Romeo at the San Juan Gospel Hall in Manila. After we'd become acquainted he would go with me sometimes to show *You Can't Win.*

"We were teaching in a Christian school in one of the tribal areas in Luzon," he explained, "but they had to close because of the persecution. We heard the Philippine Missionary Fellowship was sending workers to King's, so we came here to work as missionaries."

These were the kind of guests we liked best at the Barker Hotel. "Send us all You can, Lord," I prayed.

From its inception our organization was to be not only Philippine-based, but also of and for Filipinos. I guess the Lord was in that ideal, because He has kept us to it no matter how hard we have tried to recruit Americans to come over and help us. A number have come and given a few months, or years, but no permanent assistants have come from the States.

The first short-termers were Russel and Ethel Gottier. They joined us in the Barker Hotel, full of faith and enthusiasm and great confidence the Lord had led them to Mindanao. Russel was a large, handsome man with a dry sense of humor, who entertained the whole family with stories of how the Lord had worked in his life. Ethel was his perfect counterpart, always willing to laugh again at some story she had no doubt heard many times before.

The Gottiers arrived in the fall of 1959, shortly after Mary Beth had left for school. I'm sure the timing was of the Lord, for the house always seemed empty without our little tomboy running around. Just when we needed it, they brought laughter into our home—laughter and a sense of commitment that was beautiful to see, for they never complained about anything. Whenever problems would arise, Russel would break out singing, "Oh, this is like heaven to me!"

Well into middle age, they had sold a brand new ranch-style home in Ohio, left three grown sons, and started out to serve the Lord with the courage and optimism often associated only with the young. They were surely young in spirit, attitude, and willingness to serve the Lord no matter how lowly the task.

Russel set out to build a two-story frame building with a shop downstairs for our industrial course and living quarters upstairs. When word came we were to be joined by another couple with four children, we started praying the building would go up quickly, because we didn't know how we could fit six more into our house.

Adjusting to the heat of the tropics was difficult for Russel. He couldn't always work at the pace he would have liked, but he never wasted time. He was the most outstanding prayer warrior we'd ever had. Knowing this deeply spiritual man was on his knees praying for a situation gave me the peace of mind I needed to tackle the difficulties that pop up daily when you are dealing with so many people.

When Wayne and Donna Doll and their children arrived the first of November, the shop was not finished. Joy and Johnny had instant playmates, and we were faced with a problem more serious than the crowded conditions. We were going to have to start some kind of a school for missionary children. We were all determined that our children's education would not suffer. Since Ethel Gottier was an elementary teacher, she volunteered to start teaching Joy and the older Doll children by the Calvert correspondence system. We hoped more missionary families would join us and envisioned a school for missionary children in the south of Mindanao developing not only for ourselves but for the children of other mission groups as well.

When the shop building was finally finished, the space above was divided into two apartments, and we had a little more elbow room. Of course, we still had other visitors. Among our favorites were Vivian Forsberg, the young Wycliffe translator we had met at our commissioning service, and her two partners, Lillian Underwood and Doris Porter. They would often spend the night with us when they were traveling back and forth from their tribal assignment to the Wycliffe headquarters in Nasali, Bukidnon. Wycliffe's base was only fifteen miles from where Mary Beth was in school, and they would carry letters and packages to and from our daughter.

"We have some young men who will soon be ready for high school," Lillian informed us on one visit. "Could we enroll them at King's? It will be difficult for them to leave their own culture to come down here with all the Illoncanos and Ilongos, but this is the nearest Christian school."

"Oh, we'll look out for them," I promised. "We'll be glad to have some T'Boli students."

"Or you could just start another school, up in the mountains," she teased. I hoped she was teasing.

"What a thought!" I muttered. "We have such a problem now trying to get teachers for two schools with growing enrollments. How could we ever manage a third? Especially in such a remote location."

"It might be something to think of for the future," she added seriously. "The government estimates there are about a hundred fifty thousand T'Bolis in the mountains. Someday there will be roads into the area, and that will mean even more settlers will be moving into areas traditionally belonging to the T'Bolis. Civilization is coming whether they want it or not. We're trying to prepare them for the inevitable."

Lillian had given me something to think about. It was too implausible to mention, but deep within me I felt a desire to help these people, too. Maybe someday.

"Why don't you come up to Sinalon and visit us?" The invitation was given with a smile, and the inflection in her voice also made it a bit of a challenge. I seemed to remember Marilee warning me one time about praying for more challenges.

Of all the visitors we've had at the Barker Hotel, one "guest" was always the most special. Whenever Mary Beth came home from school she became the star attraction. Her Thanksgiving vacation was extended to include Christmas and New Year's, since travel is so time-consuming. This schedule meant she just missed being home for her ninth birthday, but we had a very special present waiting for her when she did return, a horse.

Star was just a mountain horse, not much larger than a Shetland pony and just as cute. Mary Beth had read *Black Beauty* and all the other horse stories children love, but she had never ridden a horse until she got Star. We were thankful he was very patient and gentle with her, and they sort of taught each other. She would lead him over to a bench, climb on his back, and off they'd go. She had a bridle, but rode him bareback.

Since there were no sidewalks or streets, and animals were allowed to run loose, she had plenty of space to ride him. More important, he became her friend and companion. He'd let her slide down his neck, down his tail, crawl between his legs, anything. If she fell off, he'd stop and wait for her. We were pleased with the animal, who made friends with Dutchess, and proud of our daughter for she demonstrated what a tough, determined kid she had become. Also, she was very unselfish about her prize possession and would give her sister and brother and all the neighborhood children turns.

Of course Johnny, being my son, preferred to ride a tractor rather than a horse. That little fellow was really showing a natural mechanical bent. He knew the names of all my tools, and if I sent him for a 7/16th wrench, he'd pick out just the right size. His delight was to ride in the red pickup truck with me to the fields and watch the tractors and combines at work.

The Barker kids were all well-known in our little backwater town. When Johnny, Joy, or Mary Beth rode around with me, everyone would smile at them and wave. I believe Johnny was better known than the mayor, because people would call out, "Hi, Johnny," as we passed. All of this made our kids feel they belonged.

They were all adventuresome and ready to try anything. Occasionally we had a little more adventure than we expected—like the evening I took the girls with me to Kalawag for the Christmas party marking the end of school before the holidays. It was a beautiful evening, and the stars were twinkling brightly as they do near the equator, so I decided instead of taking the short rough road home, I'd take the longer rough road since it was graveled and not so dusty.

About halfway home we had to cross a wooden bridge, but as I neared it, I realized it was under water. It must have been raining up in the mountains, a strong rain, because normally this wasn't even a creek. Most of the time it was dry, and at the most it was just a trickle of water.

I pulled up, and then a big delivery truck came up behind me. We both left our lights on, and the driver and I waded out onto the bridge to check the water level. It was only about six inches deep. "Must have been a flash flood up in the mountains," I said.

"Yes, but I think it's OK," he responded.

"Well, I don't know. There is a lower place on the other side of the bridge there."

"Well, you go ahead, and if you don't make it, I'll push you through."

That sounded like a sensible suggestion, so I tried to cross. All was fine until we got off on the other side where the road dipped downward. I noticed the water was getting deeper and deeper. Finally it got too deep, and the engine drowned out. There we sat with swift water swirling around us. True to his word, the trucker came in to push us out, but his engine drowned out also. So we were both stranded out there in the middle of the night.

Water began coming inside the truck. I realized it was getting deeper, so I got the girls out and put them in the bed of the truck, which was higher. I went back for my briefcase and then joined them. The water kept rising, and we crawled on top of the cab. After an hour or so, I was really getting concerned. After all, I had my two little girls to protect, and the water was getting higher and higher.

"It isn't getting any better, Daddy," Mary Beth announced. "What are we going to do?"

"We'll just pray, and the Lord will take care of us," I tried to reassure them.

"That's right. He took care of Dutchess for us that time, didn't He?" Joy reminded us with the beautiful faith of a six-year-old.

After we'd been about two hours on the top of the cab, the water began to recede. It was the dead of night before it was safe to get down, and I hoped Marilee wasn't too worried about us. Joy's shoes had floated away, so I carried her and held onto Mary Beth's hand as we made our way in the dark to the home of a jeep driver we knew. It was a six-mile hike, but they didn't complain a bit. Just another little adventure in the life of a missionary kid.

After the holidays, it was my turn to accompany Mary Beth to school. Malaybalay was only about 150 miles north of Marbel, but the roads were really rugged. The bus trip to the school was never less than twenty-four hours. Often there would be mud slides or construction going on in the mountains, and that made it a test of endurance. The mud would get so deep in places that the bus would just stop and wait until the next morning when a bulldozer would come and drag it through. It wasn't unusual for a dozen or even two dozen trucks to be lined up, waiting to be pulled out of the mud.

Then I had to tell her good-bye. Again. This was always difficult, for her days with us always flew by too quickly. Perhaps the separations that missionaries have to face makes us realize just how precious our children are. I hope it makes us more apt to take full advantage of the time we do have with them. For children truly are just "guests" in our homes. The Lord lends them to us for a little while, and then they are gone.

Another frequent visitor was Pop Weaver. James Oscar Weaver is one of those people who can truly be called a "character," and a very interesting one at that. The small, wiry former chief boilertender in the Navy had been dumped off in the Philippines after the war, liked it, and stayed. He and his Filipina wife, Mary, had a farm in Barrio 10 not far from the airport in Surallah and another plot of land up in the mountains among the T'Boli, where they had a store.

Pop was liable to show up at any time. He'd eat a meal or maybe two, perhaps spend the night, and then he'd be off again. He had a sort of restless spirit that is often characteristic of a man without Christ. A hard drinker, he made clear that he wanted to be friends with the only American family in the vicinity, but he was not to be preached to. I'm just as hardheaded as he is, so I made my position clear also. Without preaching, I let him know that the only reason we were in the Philippines was to have a spiritual ministry.

"I could be a farmer back in Kansas," I reminded him once. "Matter of fact, we don't get any income for our labor here. We are supported by a group of faithful friends and churches back in the States. All the profit from the farms and the cannery and the lime factory, if it ever gets to the place where it is making any money, goes into the schools."

"Well, then. Why don't you do something for the T'Boli?" he cracked. This was an oft repeated suggestion, for he truly was concerned about the welfare of the mountain people.

"Pop, it just isn't that easy. We'd love to start a work up there, but we have no capital for land and no teachers to spare. The work at King's and Kalawag is just getting going. Perhaps someday. We do have four T'Boli boys enrolled now. The Wycliffe translators sent them down here."

"Yes, but there are so many more up there. Bright young people who need an education. A little bit of your religion might not hurt them either. They have some rather unusual practices. Like marrying off the girls at ten. Many men have a number of wives, and they're little more than slaves. You should do something."

"Well, I'll pray about it," was all I could promise.

"You know, there's an American woman living up on Lake Sebu with the T'Boli, doing some missionary work."

"Really? By herself? What mission is she with?"

"Nobody, that I know of. The way I hear it, she was a missionary who was stranded in Mindanao during the war. Hid from the Japanese in the mountains and married a T'Boli man. After the war they went to the States for a time, but when she wanted to return here, he refused. I get the impression he has some sort of mental problem. Anyway, she's up there with her two kids. She's sent some T'Boli boys away to get some schooling and now has a little church going."

"How did you meet her?"

"Why, Jerry. You know I know everybody!" he cackled, slapping his hand on his bony knee. "When she went to the States for a visit a few years ago, she asked me to stay on her property and take care of it for her. We were pretty good friends by that time, so when she asked me how much I'd charge, I said, "Every once in while, you

send me a box with some candy and cake in it." She laughed, but
every once in a while I'd get a big box with a cake mix and some
candy. So I took care of the land, and the pastor took care of the
church.

"Mrs. Arroz is quite a woman," Pop declared. "Next time she
climbs down out of the mountains for supplies, I'll bring her by to
meet you."

True to his word, a few weeks later, he showed up with a large,
smiling American woman with her son and daughter in tow. Elsie
Arroz and Marilee were soon talking about their children. Paul was
older than our Mary Beth, and Grace about the same age.

"I have two concerns," the pioneer missionary confided to us. "I've
invested a decade of my life with the T'Boli people and have seen
some fruit for my labor. I want to stay with them and continue my
ministry, but at the same time I am concerned about my children.
I'm afraid I've neglected their education."

This opened a long discussion, for Marilee and I could empathize.
Finally we suggested, "You can send your children down here. Paul
can go to King's, and Grace can study the Calvert method with our
children here."

"But where will Grace stay? She's too young to live in a dormitory."

I looked at Marilee, and she shrugged. "She can stay with us. We
can always make room for one more."

Well, those kids moved down from the mountains, but getting the
mountains out of the kids was another matter. They really had a
difficult time adjusting to our civilized ways. Their teeth were bad,
and Grace kept us up more than one night with a toothache. Marilee
took her back and forth to the dentist to get them fixed, but the
youngster didn't seem to appreciate this in the least.

When her shoes fell apart, we gave her some we had purchased
for our own children. Mrs. Gottier displayed an extreme amount of
patience with her. Grace just couldn't sit still and concentrate. Since
our little elementary school had started late, they were trying to push
ahead as rapidly as possible to make up for lost time so that they
would be on schedule the next year, but one uncooperative student
made it hard for everyone.

Mrs. Arroz was very understanding. "I'll have to come up with
another solution," she said. "The only other thing I can think of is
to take them to the American Baptist school in Ilo-Ilo City. I could
take a group of T'Boli kids with me, and they could further their

education there and perhaps come back and be missionaries to their own people."

She wrote off to the school and made arrangements, and soon she and her children and about fifteen T'Bolis left for the island of Paney.

"Just think," I teased Marilee later. "Here you sometimes worry about not having things nice enough for visitors, and we ran off one because she couldn't adjust to our modern living."

"Modern living?" she snorted. "Here we are eating sardines and rice. Dirt floor in the kitchen, no refrigeration or electricity. You call that modern living?"

"To those mountain kids it is. Don't take it too hard. When you have as many guests as we do, you can't expect to please them all. I still think you have the gift of hospitality."

Boys' dorm in
1961. Still in
use in 1983.

Inside the girls' dorm.

Vocational building at King's Institute.

The Barkers (clockwise) — Marilee, Joy, Mary Beth, Jared, Jimmy, Johnny, Jabe.

John Sycip and Jared Barker — Co-founders of PEEI.

The original Barker residence, "the Barker Hotel," later became the college canteen.

Making some of the first cement blocks for construction at the college.

Lowering corn into sterilizer at the cannery.

The poultry houses.

Overturned weapons
carrier after the
accident on the road to
Lake Sebu.

Teacher's cottage
at Lake Sebu.

Market store in rural Muslim community.

John Deere
tractor arriving
at Subic Bay.

Doing medical
check-ups on
T'Boli school
children.

Manobo house at Lagubang.

5
Opportunities Unlimited

PEEI has never had a lack of opportunities. We have at times been overwhelmed by so many of them and concerned how we could best take advantage of them. In the summer of 1960 there was one we didn't want to miss. The Taylor University basketball-playing preachers, called "Venture for Victory," were touring the Philippines, and we wanted them in Cotabato.

The Philippine Crusade mission was managing the team, and they scheduled them in a number of towns in our area. This was a fun thing, and the people turned out in droves. The team would play local teams, and of course everyone expected them to win, especially since they were two feet taller than the Filipino high school boys. Rather than just a competition, they would turn it into a teaching opportunity, displaying many new techniques for the youngsters.

They showed off their expertise, rather like the Harlem Globe Trotters do, then they'd fumble, or fall down, or do something silly, and the crowd would just roar to see those big Americanos goofing off. They let the other team get some points, and even get ahead for a while, but they always won. Then at halftime they had a program. They set up an amplifier, gave testimonies, and sang a few songs. Afterward they handed out tracts inviting the Filipinos to take a Bible correspondence course.

This was an effective ministry and reached many who would never go to a church. We felt especially privileged to keep them in our home while they were in our area. They were great favorites with our kids, and the basketball players seemed to enjoy being with American youngsters for a time.

We arrived home after a game in Marbel to find total confusion. "Sir, Mary Beth has been bitten by a rabid dog!" the totally distraught house girl announced.

"Let me see the bite," Marilee demanded, turning nurse again. Mary Beth held out her hand, and she had indeed been bitten between her thumb and forefinger. "How do you know the dog had rabies?" she asked the crowd of neighbors who had gathered.

"We saw it! We saw it!" a number of them insisted.

"But Mary Beth, you and Joy were supposed to be upstairs taking a nap. How could this have happened?"

Mary Beth hung her head while she was explaining, but she didn't seem the least bit repentant. "We didn't want to wait until tonight to see the team play," she explained. "So we crawled out the window onto the roof and down the jackfruit tree."

This confession amused the neighbors and the basketball players, but not her mother and me. Joy was always such a good little girl. She tried so hard to please us, but Mary Beth was always getting into trouble.

"You'll have to have a series of rabies shots," Marilee pronounced. "I think that will be punishment enough."

Johnny came running up to the tallest of the players and looked up at him as if he were a towering tree. I'd got used to feeling tall, since at five feet ten I'm about half a foot taller than the average Filipino male, but these guys made me feel like a pygmy. This athlete ruffled Johnny's hair, bent down, and asked him, "Well, what are you going to be when you grow up?"

"A pilot," he proclaimed.

"A pilot?" I echoed. "Where did you ever get that idea? I thought you wanted to be a farmer/mechanic?"

"Oh, he has a little book that he likes that is all about airplanes," Marilee explained.

Kids can come up with the most unusual ideas, but that was just an indication to me how important early influences are to them. As missionary kids they missed out on many things kids in the States take for granted, but we believed that these were overshadowed by opportunities like getting to know those fine young men from Venture for Victory.

Sometimes opportunities come as a result of leaping out in faith. By the beginning of 1962 our continuing need for Christian teachers made us realize that we needed to have a college so we could train some of the young people won to Christ through our school ministry to become a part of the ongoing work. When we sent in an application to the government for opening the first year of a new college, we had neither equipment nor qualified personnel. Yet we believed that if the Lord supplied the permit, He would surely supply the other necessities.

If I thought about a college too much, I'd get a little uneasy feeling in my stomach. We were already so overextended. We had the farms going, keeping two schools afloat. The cannery was running full blast, and we were shipping over two hundred cases of corn a week. Our custom service was not only making a profit but was also providing a valuable service to local farmers who were able to plant much larger crops because of the mechanized assistance. And the lime factory—well, it was still operating because of John's insistence, but it was certainly a losing proposition. We also had a continuing building program going on. Most of these were local-type construction, but we'd never finish one structure before another was needed.

You'd think that anyone with good sense wouldn't want to take on added responsibilities, but we had organized as the Philippine Evangelical Enterprises, and that plural just kept taking on more emphasis. Our family was also growing, and time was nearing for the delivery of Johnny's little brother. He kept insisting it was going to be a brother, "because we already have two girls." He felt strongly that the family should be evened out.

Marilee had to spend most of two months in bed before the birth. Then she flew to Malaybalay in Bukidnon so she could deliver at the Bethel Baptist Clinic there. We had scheduled our vacation for this time, so I followed with Mary Beth, Joy, and Johnny in the truck. We spent our vacation in nearby Nasuli, the cool, quiet, mountain base camp of the Wycliffe translators. Those folks know how to pick a location!

At 11:00 P.M. on April 15, Marilee decided it was time to drive to the clinic, and we bounced over the eleven miles of bumpy, mountain roads as fast as I dared. At 4:00 A.M. Johnny's little brother gave his first cry. We named him Jared William Barker, Jr. Then it seemed that Jared was too dignified a name for such a little bit of humanity, and since I was already called Jerry, the name Jabe evolved.

Shortly after we returned to our little bungalow in Marbel, we received permission to begin the first year of a liberal arts college course. I plunged into the work. The first week of June we had teachers' orientation and a retreat in preparation for the coming school year. Marilee kept telling me that Jabe wasn't doing well. He had diarrhea, he wasn't eating well, he wasn't sleeping. That was woman's work. I was busy with important matters and left the baby tending to her.

Jabe was six weeks old when Marilee convinced me she had to take him to a hospital to get treatment. I put them on the plane to Davao so he could be cared for at the Brokenshire Hospital. The Lord is really gracious, because I didn't realize just how sick my little son was and didn't pray as much as I would have if I'd known. It was three weeks later when they returned home that I learned just how close we had come to losing the little one we had waited for so long.

"When I got there the director of the hospital, Dr. Bruce, examined him," Marilee told me. "He looked at him and said, 'I don't know what we can do, but we'll try to save him.' I didn't know what to do. I didn't know anyone in Davao. I couldn't even call you and have people pray."

"I just had to talk to someone. Finally I remembered Dr. Ling, a Chinese eye specialist we had heard was Christian. I called him, and he and his wife came over to be with me. They were such a blessing. I'm just so thankful the Lord provided them for me when I needed them.

"Jabe was in critical condition for so long. I'd sit by his bed and pray. I'd look at him lying there, fighting to live, and think of the two months I'd spent in bed so we could keep him. I remembered how hard the delivery had been. It just seemed that he was such a special little guy, a miracle baby from the start.

"One night he was crying so pitifully, and I picked him up and walked him, and I prayed, 'Well, Lord, he's Yours. You know how much I love him, but if You want him, take him.'

"The turning point came that night. I heard this sort of restful little sigh, and I looked at him, and he looked right at me and smiled. It was the most beautiful smile. As if he were saying, 'It's OK, Mom.'"

I felt bad that I hadn't been with my wife during that crisis, but I was so thankful that the Lord had been with her and little Jabe. He was still a sickly little guy and needed lots of special care, but she had an amazing amount of patience with him.

Then there were the medical bills. It's times like this when living by faith can really be exciting. We had no guaranteed income—never knew what would come in in any given month. But that month there were extra gifts. Just enough to care for the bills. This has happened so many times over the years that we wouldn't think of going on salary. The Lord knows our needs.

Experiences like that make me all the more eager to share His goodness with everyone. I was in Tupi, a little rural town near one of our farms, when I thought of Magdalena, the young girl who had worked so hard to finish high school. I hadn't heard what she was doing since graduation, so I stopped by her house. I was disappointed to find that she was not continuing her education but was back working in the fields.

"There is no money at all for me to study," she confided.

"Would you like to begin college at Kalawag?"

"Oh sir, I would like to so very much. I would work so hard."

"I know you are a good worker, Mags. There is a teacher who needs a house girl—"

"Oh, I will be the one, sir," she exclaimed. "I will be the one to cook for her, and wash, and clean. I will do it. If I can just get my education. Someday I want to be a teacher."

The arrangements were made, and Mags got her opportunity. It was rewarding to see her eagerness, yet it made me sad to think of how many young Filipino boys and girls still had no such opportunity to change their futures.

"I've got a generator in Manila for you," John Sycip announced one weekend while he was staying with us. "I'm going to ship it down to you so you can have electricity here."

This was certainly an unexpected opportunity. "Where did you get it, John?" I asked.

"Well, Wycliffe needed one for their base in Nasuli, so they bought two used ones from the US military. Surplus stuff. They got two so that if one needed repairs they could use the second one for parts. They brought them into my shop and asked me to check them out and see if I could get one in usable condition. Well, one was virtually unused and in excellent condition. So they told me we could use the other one until they needed it."

"Well, that's really generous of them. What kind is it?"

"Oh, it's a thirty-kilowatt diesel."

"A thirty-kilowatt diesel! John, thirty kilowatts is big enough for the whole town of Marbel. Besides, I've never maintained a diesel generator in my life. What would we do with a thing that size anyway?"

"Now Jerry, I've heard you say that if the Lord provides a thing it must be for a purpose. So He's provided this generator. He must have some plan for it."

I couldn't argue with logic like that, so we waited for the arrival of our generator. It was shipped to General Santos and brought over by truck. It filled the whole bed of a two-ton truck. It was about 10 feet long by 4 feet wide and stood over 5 feet tall—a monstrous thing.

The obvious place for it was the center of the campus so we could run wires to each of the buildings. So we positioned it right behind the toilet. I must digress to explain that having the toilet in the center of the campus was not my idea. It had been there before we arrived. It wasn't the most esthetic location, but it was handy—practical— right next to the huge tamarind tree.

I messed around with the generator until I learned to start it. And when it started up, everyone knew it. Was it ever noisy. But it worked, and we began wiring the campus. This immediately extended the time we could use our facilities and made it possible for me to read in bed when I found it difficult to sleep.

The generator was a convenience, but it was just so much more power than we needed. I couldn't see how we would ever need all that electricity. We would have to build a skyscraper to utilize all that power. The Lord had provided it, so we took it, but I wished He had provided an overabundance of manpower instead. The Gottiers had finished their two years of service and had left. The Dolls would be leaving soon. A young couple named Cates had come with their little girl, and Mrs. Cates was now teaching the missionary children, but our shortage of teachers continued to grow in proportion to the ever-increasing enrollments at the schools.

We now had close to 900 students counting the 90 students in the college department. Kalawag High had 425 and King's Institute about 350. With a staff of 36 teachers, the pupil/teacher ratio was somewhat less than ideal.

Every time I'd start feeling discouraged, the Lord would provide an additional boost. That year it came in the form of a letter from William Layda. William was the skinny little fellow who had accepted Christ on my first survey trip to Mindanao. After graduating from our high school, he had gone to FEBIA, a Bible school in Manila. His letter was such a glowing report of his continued walk with the Lord that it inspired me. Perhaps he would come back to Mindanao to help us. Surely the Lord had demonstrated that He is in the business of supplying power. We just have to tap into the source.

One of our concerns during this time was a work among the T'Boli people. Pop Weaver kept nagging at me about the need for a school in the mountains, and the Wycliffe people encouraged us to keep the possibility alive. With the new college department started, this seemed another impossibility, for there was no way we could afford to buy land.

"I'll give PEEI all my land at Lake Sebu, if you will establish a school there," Mrs. Arroz promised. "I've got to do something for my children, but my heart is still with the T'Bolis, and I can't just forget them."

The experiment at the school in Ilo-Ilo hadn't worked. Her kids couldn't adjust there, and neither could the T'Bolis she had taken with her. She realized she was going to have to return to the States because of her youngsters. "The need for a school at Lake Sebu has been proved by those I've sent out for an education. They become aculturated to civilization and don't want to return and help their people. Of all those who have gone out, only two are back trying to be missionaries to their own people."

Now this was an opportunity! We had two T'Boli boys studying in the college with the goal of becoming teachers. The Wycliffe people had material translated and primers available that would be of great assistance in operating a new school. The property in Lake Sebu was in the opposite direction from the translators' station in Sinalon, so there would be no competition. Wycliffe didn't compete anyway—they always sought to serve the evangelical missions.

Before any intelligent decision could be made, a survey trip had to be taken. With four teachers, a student, and a Peace Corps worker, I hiked up to Lake Sebu on a Thanksgiving afternoon. Because it was the dry period, our jeep was able to ford several of the rivers and climb the path almost halfway. The trail was good, so we were able to hike to Pop Weaver's place in three hours.

Pop's two sons had married and were living close to Pop and Mary's house, so they had a little settlement there by their store. We made this our headquarters and spent the night. The next morning we took the boat Mrs. Arroz had left and rowed across the lake. Lake Sebu is actually three lakes with 100-foot falls at the outlet. Incredibly beautiful. The larger, center lake is completely surrounded by mountains with various peaks protruding from the water forming five small islands. The mountainsides surrounding the lakes were covered with virgin forest and native products for building.

We landed on the far side of the long lake and began hiking toward

Mrs. Arroz's forty acres. The land was low there and very muddy.
Because of the water and the tall grass it was a miserable place to
hike. Our feet would sink into the ooze and make a suction noise
each time we pulled a foot out. There was a good deal of forest
around so it was very damp. The gnats were starving to death and
made a feast of us.

Altogether, it was quite debatable whether we could ever farm this
land or make use of it for a school or anything else. After we had
hiked quite a way, the land rose up out of the swamp, and the going
got easier. Finally we came to Mrs. Arroz's big, native house with its
bamboo walls and grass roof.

It was sad to see the big country home of native materials, where
she had worked so hard and tried so long, and to think she had had
to give up. She had done her best to make this a real home. There
were orchids growing from the roof, and I could see where she had
her medical work and where she had been teaching her children. It
made me cry to see how hard this kind, generous woman had worked.
For twelve years she had sacrificed to bring these people the gospel.
And now this empty house was all that was left.

There was a strong sentimental pull to try to establish a school
there just because I admired Mrs. Arroz, but that couldn't be the
basis for the decision. We decided to go back across the lake to a
more comfortable site and sit down and discuss the pros and cons
of the situation.

The cons came quickly. The land was not on the lake. Bringing
in supplies to a place like that would be extremely difficult even
during the dry season. There were supposed to be 7,000 families
living near the lake, but her land was in a sort of isolated place. It
would be necessary to ferry all personnel and supplies across the
lake, which was so deep we were told it was bottomless. And it was
questionable whether the land would be usable for farming.

The pros: It was being offered to us free, and there was my old
philosophy about the Lord's not giving you a thing unless He had
a purpose for it. There was the spiritual heritage and the years of
prayer that Mrs. Arroz had invested in the land to consider, yet we
had to wonder. Did we really want this land?

"We could use the land for camping and retreats," one of the
teachers suggested. "This would certainly be away from it all."

"Yes, but we were offered the land on the provision we establish
a school on it," I reminded them.

"Well, there are not many settlers on that side of the lake," Pop
Weaver injected.

"That's not surprising." I snorted. "The settlers don't want it. There's no transportation, no roads, no lakefront, few people. Why would they want land over there?"

"Well, before you make up your mind, you should talk to some of the T'Bolis," he insisted.

We hiked around, visiting various villages, talking to the *datus*, the tribal leaders, and we visited in a number of T'Boli homes. Their reaction was unanimous. They wanted us. They almost begged us to come and establish a school for their children.

We could come to but one conclusion. There were so many negatives and so few advantages that it was an impossibility, humanly speaking. But we'd found God seems to major in accomplishing things that are impossible without Him. We said, "Yes. We will do it."

We knew it would take time before we could obtain an official government permit for a school at Lake Sebu, but we started making plans anyway. I wrote Mrs. Arroz telling her of our plans, and that was one letter I enjoyed writing.

"We hope to put up a building within the next few weeks that could be used as a camp," I explained. "This could also be used as a residence and possibly as a temporary school. We plan to have a student retreat there in a few months. As soon as workers and teachers are available we will start some classes. Before the Bureau of Private Schools will grant us a permit, we must prove ownership of the land. Therefore, it is imperative we settle the question of title to the land as soon as possible."

Our first camping trip to Lake Sebu was quite an experience. With nearly a hundred students and teachers we were quite a mass of humanity climbing the side of that mountain. We hired T'Boli carriers to help with the baggage, but since we had to bring in all our equipment, food, bedding, and clothing we still all had to carry our share.

When we got to the lake we hired *banka*s, hollowed-out logs the T'Boli use for canoes. They were so unstable we couldn't trust them to ferry our students across the "bottomless" lake, so we lashed five together into a raftlike affair that was cumbersome but safe. We made two trips with about fifty on this raft each trip.

On the far side of the lake, we picked up our burdens and sloshed through the mud to the Arroz house. We were puffing along, and I began to reconsider Johnny's idea of being a pilot. It wouldn't be much trouble to make a landing strip up here, and it would sure save a lot of time and effort. My eight-year-old son was keeping up

with the rest of the crew, so I called out, "Hey, Johnny. You still
want to be a pilot?"

"Of course," he replied, bobbing his crew cut. "I could fly up here
easy, huh?" Smart kid. He knew just what I was thinking.

"I tell you what, son. You grow up and become a pilot, and we'll
start praying for the Lord to provide a plane."

About that time we broke through the tall grass and came upon
the house. The bamboo structure was falling in, and the T'Bolis had
been using the bamboo for firewood. It was a sad sight, and yet the
excitement of the campers brought a new atmosphere to the clearing,
a feeling of anticipation that was a portent of things of come. Surely
the Lord had given us this opportunity for a purpose.

6
Troubles and Trials

Mindanao in the early 1960s was still very much a frontier territory, and just as early settlers in our own western frontier days faced certain dangers, we too knew our share of growing pains. There were unscrupulous individuals who were out to benefit themselves even if it meant harming those who got in the way. As in every society there were those who were lawless and ruthless.

Our first serious confrontation came over at Kalawag. Agriculturist Pete Cargas and his Bible-teacher wife, Avelina, were living in a native house near the campus with their three small children and a couple of relatives who were students at the school. One morning Pete and Avelina greeted me in quite an agitated state, both talking at once.

"Oh, sir," Pete began. "You have to move us from this place. We can stay here no longer. It is not safe."

"We were robbed!" exclaimed Avelina. "There were three of them. They had weapons. We were so scared!"

"We can no longer live here with our babies," Pete continued. "We want to transfer to Marbel. We will teach at King's."

"Whoa," I told them. "Calm down and tell me just what happened. One at a time."

"You know I am treasurer of the school," Avelina began. "I have been collecting money for tuitions because this is examination week. Yesterday is the last day of collections. Last night, after dark, we were in our home when my assistant came to bring me the last of the monies, so I opened our door to her. She was followed by robbers!

"Our babies were in the other room, asleep. Pete's nephew and my sister were in there with them, and so was the money. The robbers forced us to lie down on our stomachs and yelled, 'We want the money.' While we were getting down on the floor, the young people grabbed the money and climbed out a window and ran for the school.

"The men were so angry! We were certain they were going to kill us all, but when the principal was told what had happened he began ringing the school bell. The noise frightened the men away."

Transfering the Cargases to King's Institute was no problem, but that didn't help matters any at Kalawag. I was especially concerned for the single teachers who lived in a dorm some distance from the campus. This teachers' dorm had originally been built with the hope that we could have a resident missionary family assigned to that school, since I couldn't be in both places at once. This is a need that has still not been filled.

Our concern was deepened by the next incident. We had hired a student to act as "technician" and turn off the generator after evening classes were over at the college. This made him the last man on campus each night. He was accosted by a group of hooligans after performing his duties one night, forced into a banana grove, and beaten badly while the ringleader held him at gunpoint. They were trying to force him to summon one of the lady teachers out into the night, but he refused. When a group of carolers began singing in the teachers' dorm, they realized there were too many people around and left.

There was a good deal of unrest in the whole area about that time because of warring political factions embattled in an election campaign. We felt more secure in Marbel, because it was a larger community, but we were to learn that we were not immune.

We were awakened the night after the election by shouts, "The market is on fire! The market is on fire!" I jumped into some clothes and hurried to the market, about a mile from the campus. The market is strategic to our little town because it is the major source of income in the valley. For an ousted official to take revenge there was no better way than to destroy the heart of the town income.

The market is really a series of little stalls covered by a general roof. People rent space and then build their own facilities. All of this, of course, was of bamboo, and it was really burning fast. With the only available water coming in trucks, the volunteer firemen didn't have much of a chance. The merchants were hauling out their wares as quickly as possible.

I noticed a man running across the roof carrying the mayor's typewriter. The mayor was a close friend of mine, so I figured I'd try to help save his equipment. "Here, let me hold that for you while you climb down," I told this fellow. He got down, grabbed the typewriter out of my hands, and dashed off. I was greatly chagrined when it dawned on me that this fellow wasn't saving the mayor's property. He was stealing it. And I'd helped him!

By the light of dawn the next morning our town was in shambles. Not only the market, but the municipal building, the post office, and about a third of the business district had gone up in flames. The government sent in the army to control the further threats of violence, which included threats to all the schools in the area.

Senseless destruction like this is difficult to understand, yet it made us all realize just how basically insecure people are who trust in material possessions, which can all be destroyed in a night. Our confidence had to be in the Lord. He is our only real security, our only source of protection.

It is quite possible to precipitate trouble even though you are completely innocent and have the most altruistic motives for your actions. When the principal from Kalawag High School, Mr. Eglesia, came to me with a sad story about how his nephew had been unfairly incarcerated, I believed him.

"He's innocent, Mr. Barker," he assured me with a pleading tone. "He's innocent, and yet his family suffers. He has all these children, and no one to feed them. He needs to get out of jail so he can work and support his family."

So I went with Mr. Eglesia to the jail and vouched for his nephew, who was called Boy, and got him out on bail. I even gave him a job over on a farm we were working at that time between Isulan and Tacurong. Boy was to live on the farm as well as work there, and I thought that was the end of the problem. Was I ever naive.

Surprisingly, the difficulties started with the uncle. Shortly after the death of his wife, the principal took up with one of our teachers who was young enough to be his daughter. They left with funds belonging to the school and got married. He then started a smear campaign to try to destroy the work. He succeeded in influencing the dean of the college to resign, and having three key employees gone made quite a hole in our staff, but the worst thing was the rumor campaign that they started. It was said that the schools would not open next term, that they had been sold, that all the teachers had left. Despite all this, we had record enrollments for the next term.

When this plan was thwarted, he tried to confiscate all our leased land. Then the intimidations began. This campaign was directed by his staunch supporter, his nephew, Boy. He gathered a gang of ruffians, about fifteen or twenty of them, and they made life miserable for anyone who got in their way. We began getting reports of his blocking the road so people couldn't get to the school. Then we heard stories of his holding up places of business.

I went to the authorities for help and was told he had been in jail on suspicion of murdering two men. He was supposed to have been involved in a boat piracy in which the captain and the first mate were both killed. And I had got him out of jail! Now it seemed the local authorities were frightened of him too, and could do nothing to stop him.

I was in the office at Kalawag when we had our first personal confrontation. He pointed a gun at me and announced, "I'm going to shoot you!" The place was full of students and teachers, and everyone scattered. Fast. Some of them told me later that they had gone outside to pray. I'm glad they did.

He was drunk, and I couldn't understand the torrent of words he unleashed at me. He was talking in Ilongo, but I got enough of it to understand that he had come to kill me. He had his gang outside guarding the place, so no one could come to rescue me. I just sat there and listened, as quietly and calmly as possible.

He raved on and on, repeating himself, as drunks are prone to do. After a while he started running out of steam, and backed out, still brandishing his pistol and shouting threats. The teachers came running in, exclaiming how brave I had been. I really didn't feel all that brave; it was just a situation where there was absolutely nothing I could do but pray and trust the Lord to protect me.

We closed down the farm project where Boy had been working, and that enraged him all the more. Not only was he out of work again, but a number of his relatives had also been working there, and they too were without jobs. He became even more dangerous, holding up rice fields and stores. Every business in the vicinity was in jeopardy, but the shootings had the people so terrified that no one tried to stop him. The real power terrorists have over people is fear. Without fear they would have banded together and brought this lawlessness to an end. Instead the Moslem mayor hired Boy as a bodyguard.

I went back to the mayor. "I think that as a visitor in your country and a director of a private school, we should have a right to freedom here," I told him. "We are serving the community, and yet my life is continually being harrassed by one of your bodyguards, and I think I have a right to be protected from the government."

He didn't come right out and say he couldn't control Boy, but he sort of laughed off my complaint and suggested, "Well, probably if you would hire him as a bodyguard, he would protect you."

It seemed to me that this was developing into a Mafia-style protection racket. I wasn't about to "hire" Boy. We didn't have any extra money for a payoff, and besides, anything we earned belonged to the Lord and His work. There was too much to be done to devote so much time and energy to this criminal.

We were putting up a building at Lake Sebu at this time, making plans for the next camp and for beginning a first grade class among the T'Bolis. Tatang Bajo, our friend from the leper colony, had agreed to oversee the project and to stay on the premises to guard the equipment. He had been having some trouble with his lungs, and Marilee suggested the higher altitude and cleaner air might help him. His only complaint was that he got very cold at night. Some evenings at that elevation the temperature might get down to 70°, which might not impress anyone back in Kansas, but for a man used to the heat of the tropics, I'm sure he did feel cold.

Pastor Napila, one of the fellows Mrs. Arroz had sent to Bible school, was a great help in this project. He helped secure laborers and located materials for us. Supplies such as nails, hammers, and saws all had to be packed up. We had Star, Mary Beth's little horse, up there for Tatang to use, since he wasn't too strong and couldn't carry heavy loads or walk long distances. Mary Beth and Joy were both at school in Malaybalay at this time, and Star wasn't getting much exercise in Marbel anyway, so it was probably good for him, too.

An exciting prospect opened for us during one of my trips to Manila to meet with our board. The possibility of establishing a radio station on the King's campus was discussed with the Far East Broadcasting Company. The conclusion was that since they had a transmitter and the know-how, and PEEI had the land and the necessary generator, we would apply for a permit and frequency assignment.

The word was out that no more permits were being granted, but we figured if the Lord could provide the generator in the way He had, He certainly could overcome any difficulties we might meet in the bureaucracy.

I returned to Mindanao full of enthusiasm and was greeted with the news that one of the teachers had kicked out a student who happened to be one of Boy's gang members.

"But, sir, he was carrying a concealed weapon," Raquel Reyes informed me, pulling herself up indignantly. "He brought a knife to class. I could not permit that."

"Of course not. You did the right thing, Raquel. The boy was a troublemaker anyway, and the school will probably be better off without him. It's just that we've already seen that Boy is full of vengeance. No doubt he'll be planning some kind of revenge. We'll have to seek the Lord's guidance and protection."

When the frequency assignment came from the government we were all elated, especially John Sycip, since this had been a dream of his even before PEEI was founded. With thirty or more dialects spoken in Mindanao, radio seemed the most practical way to reach into the hinterlands of the island. Transistors were just becoming available, and their novelty made for a ready audience who would listen to anything coming over the magic boxes.

FEBC had begun making cheap little transistor radios available that were preset to their frequency. They would give them out free, and the people just had to buy the batteries, but because they were preset they heard the gospel on these little PMs—portable missionaries. I couldn't wait to get our station in operation so we could become a part of that operation.

Of course it was going to take thousands of dollars, and considering our bank account it might as well have been millions, but John insisted, "Let's start. We'll go as far as the money holds out, then trust the Lord to send more." He agreed to be responsible for raising the funds for the project. I strongly suspect that much of the money came from the Sycip family, although all financing was funneled through PEEI.

FEBC sent their experts down to make a survey and found that the perfect location for a station that would reach the most people in southern Mindanao was the southeast corner of our campus. If we had needed any added encouragement that this project was of the Lord, this certainly was it. We were told we would need a 300-foot tower to get the maximum coverage. This would be the tallest structure on the entire island. It would take men with special training to put up something like that, but I was ready to tackle the cement block building that would house the transmitter and studios.

"You know, everyone here at King's is all happy and excited about the prospect of the radio station, but I can't help but be concerned about the teachers over at Kalawag," Marilee said one evening at the dinner table. "They're stuck over there and are constantly being harrassed. I think we should do something for them."

"You're right. That is a faithful, loyal bunch over there; we should do something special for them. Any suggestions?"

She thought a bit, brightened up, and said, "We could take the stuff over there and make them some homemade ice cream. That would be a real treat for them."

"Perfect." She gathered her supplies, baby Jabe, and young Johnny, and we were climbing into the truck when one of the Moslem students dropped by. He wanted to go along for the ride, so he jumped into the back of the truck.

Just before arriving at the school there is a small river to ford. When we got to that point, a bunch of Boy's gang surrounded us.

"Boy doesn't want you coming here," one of the ruffians announced. I recognized him as the troublemaker who had been kicked out of school for carrying a knife.

"Well, we are coming across," I told him. "This is a public road, and Boy has no authority to stop me or anyone else. He doesn't own that school. We do, and he's not keeping us out."

I must have sounded pretty gruff, because they backed down and let us cross the river. We reached the campus, and I stopped while the student jumped down and opened the gate for us. After I drove through, he closed it behind him.

We walked into the administration building, and the teachers were all there, and they seemed quite frightened. "Why did you come?" they demanded. "It is dangerous for you to be here. You know Boy wants to kill you. We had gathered here to pray that they wouldn't come into the compound. They are all around."

"Well, you are all brave enough to stay here and keep the school going, we can at least come and visit you. We're going to make some ice cream." This announcement was received with more enthusiasm, because if there is one thing the people of Mindanao love, it is ice cream.

Marilee and one of the teachers, David Feliciano, went to get the ice cream freezer and supplies from the back of the truck. The teachers gathered around me and began expressing some of their fears. I think talking about the situation helped relieve the tension a bit, and I was really glad we had come.

I was beginning to wonder what was taking Marilee so long, when she came dashing in, with Jabe on one hip and talking so fast she was almost incoherent.

"Boy was out there! I went across the road to the sari-sari store to get ice, and he was there with one of his henchmen, a big, mean, scary-looking guy."

"You went across the road by yourself?"

"Well, it was just across from the campus, such a short way, and I thought all the men were down by the river, but when I got there, I saw Boy. I just tried to be nonchalant and talked to him the same as I would anyone, but that other guy kept telling him, 'Sigue. Sigue. Get her. Get her.'

"I think I was safer because I had the baby with me. I couldn't look very frightening to him. I asked him about his children and how they were doing. Then I told him, 'You know, Boy, we still love you because of Jesus. He loves you, and so do we. I know you want to kill my husband, and I don't want you to, but even if you did I would still love you because of Jesus.' He really seemed to be touched by what I said."

"Oh, Marilee, you are so sentimental. It's going to take more than that to touch the heart of a criminal like Boy. No one knows how many men he has killed. It was foolish for you to go over there. I'm just thankful you're all right."

"I don't know," she insisted. "He got this funny look on his face while I was talking to him."

A short time later the young ruffian who had been kicked out of school was found floating down the Allah River. I didn't see, but I was told he had been beheaded. There was probably some sort of an investigation, but they never found who did it.

A fellow named Byrd Brunemeier from New Tribes Mission came to stay with us to take charge of the tower construction. He laid it all out. There were three base marks for anchors, and those had to be in just the right position. He had to juggle those to just the right angle because all three are right on the boundary of the campus. It had to fit exactly. A big hole was dug in the center, and a six-foot foundation of concrete laid.

Then we had to wait for the tower construction team to come from Manila. They put the tower up in 10-feet sections. After one section was in place they anchored it with guy wires, then used a pulley and rope to draw up the next section. They'd set it down and bolt it, slide a jin pole up on that, bolt it, and pull up another section. Each section had to have all the guy wires in just the right position.

It was really interesting to watch these men working, and they had a crowd of curious onlookers at all times. This was the best show in town, and it was free. After the tower was up about 100 feet a couple of the fellows didn't want to go any higher. Dick Roland, a missionary with FEBC, who was to be our first station manager, certainly won everyone's respect as he climbed higher and higher up those steps. He had a slender, wiry body and could climb like a monkey, but he was always careful to hook up his safety belts. Seeing him up there kept me in constant prayer that the Lord would protect him—lift him up and keep him from falling.

All this took time, and we had the DXKI studio building closed in before the tower was finished. When we had to stop construction because of lack of funds, the teachers gave up their salaries because they said they wanted to have a part in the station, too.

It was about this time that Marilee reminded me one evening, "You know, it's been nearly six months since we've had any trouble from Boy or his gang."

"That's right. I've been so busy I hadn't thought about it much. We keep hearing stories of him bothering others, but he hasn't bothered us since the night—"

Marilee sat there looking smug, wearing an "I told you so" expression. "The Lord sometimes uses unusual methods for protecting us, doesn't He?" was all she said.

Most missionaries take furloughs every five years. Some missions recommend a furlough every four years for countries designated as hardship fields. We had begun getting letters from loved ones in 1963 wondering when we would be coming home since we had been in Mindanao since late 1958. But there was no way we could leave, because so many things were happening. As 1964 was drawing to a rapid close I mentioned in our prayer letter that we were completely without reserve funds to enable us to get to the States.

Marilee and I then turned the matter over to the Lord. If He wanted us to go He'd not only have to provide the funds, but also someone who could take over responsibility for the enterprises of PEEI while I was gone. Although we had many dedicated workers, there was no one who could oversee all our various projects.

One thing that encouraged all of us about the future prospects for teachers was a plan PEEI's board devised that we called "Go Now Pay Later." This was to be a revolving credit plan that would help some of our brightest students go to Christian schools for the last two years of college so they could get their degrees and come back and teach for us. They were then to pay back the fund so much a month from their salaries, and in this way the fund could be used to help others. We had five of our young people studying under this plan and were looking forward to having them come home to teach for us.

One of our enterprises hadn't worked out well—the school for missionary children. We just didn't have enough teachers to spare for so few children, so the Barker kids spent the '64-'65 school year at Faith Academy in Manila. One of our concerns was that if we did get to go on furlough, we wanted our kids to be academically prepared for the schools in Kansas.

Mary Beth was having problems adjusting to being a teenager. It was hard for me to adjust to the idea she was growing up so quickly. One of our fine young teachers became her *barcada*, her special friend. Belen Edralin, who was from a very prominent family in Luzon, had come as a missionary to her own people to serve as a teacher in Mindanao. She took time for long walks and talks with Mary Beth. The two were prayer partners, and even when Mary was away, I knew Belen was still praying for her regularly.

The last six weeks of 1964 everything started falling into place. First Glenn and Fay Jackson and their two sons made a dramatic entrance. They had had a hard trip from Manila with several unexpected delays enroute, but they finally rolled into Marbel on an old army weapons carrier. They came with excellent references, and we were glad to put them to work.

Then in December DXKI went on the air. Many important people came down from Manila, and the governor of the state of Cotabato came to help us inaugurate the station. Our town officials, no matter their religious affiliation, were proud of having a local station. It seemed everyone wanted to be in on the glory of the occasion, except for one smiling Chinese businessman who was content to take a back seat and watch. John Sycip had had more to do with the dream of a Christian radio station becoming a reality than any man there, but in his typically modest way he let others take the credit.

After only three evenings of test broadcasting we began receiving good reports from the listeners. We then began broadcasting four hours daily and seven and one half hours on Sundays. Two men came and bought all the Ilongo dialect Bibles we had in stock for themselves and their neighbors, because the Ilongo radio preacher always said, "Now open your Bibles and follow . . ." One Christian living in a remote village sold his carabao to buy a radio so his unsaved neighbors could come to his house and hear the Word of God. Another sold his rice field for the same purpose.

It is a well-established Filipino custom to share with your neighbors. Because of this, people would always play their radios at full volume to "share" with neighbors who might not have one. Since sound carries through bamboo, the neighbors would hear whether they wanted to or not. It was neat to drive down the road and hear the sound of the gospel coming from little grass homes along the way.

We were still marveling at the response from the radio station when gifts started coming in to make it possible for us to go on furlough. I'd written one paragraph in one prayer letter, but the response was heartening. Our staff also collected 700 pesos as a love gift to us. The Lord had promised to supply all our needs, and perhaps He was protecting our sanity by giving us time away from the pressures on the field.

We began planning to leave after school was out in June. The decision was made to transfer the college from Kalawag to King's in Marbel, which was a more stable environment. I felt better about having the students and faculty in this community. One of the teachers, Rachel Reyes, became my secretary and general assistant. I think she was capable of running the whole show, but in this culture it wouldn't be acceptable for a female to be in charge.

Getting ready to leave the field, even for just a year, is rather like an extremely nostalgic New Year's Eve. You can't help but look back and recount some of the events of the past term. There were the obvious highlights, the increased enrollments in the two schools we had inherited, the college, and the new school at Lake Sebu. The radio station was a real climax to the term, and yet I had to stop and be thankful for some of the things that hadn't happened. Although we'd had our share of illnesses, we were all now in reasonably good health. Johnny hadn't been seriously injured when his shirt caught in the auger of the combine, pulling him in. We'd been able to get rabies shots for Mary Beth when she'd been bitten by that dog. Baby Jabe had had more than his share of problems but was able to obtain medical assistance when it was needed. I'd had more than one gun pointed in my direction, but no triggers had been pulled. In all the traveling we'd done, in some of the roughest terrain in the world, we'd had no injury. I couldn't remember thanking the Lord very often for things that hadn't happened, but reviewing our years in Mindanao I became very aware of His protection.

7

Home Is Where the Heart Is

Kansas seemed like another world after nearly seven years in Mindanao. It was good to be home again. This furlough we stayed with Dad on his farm in Louisburg. Somehow the house reminded me of Dad. It was old, solid, square, unmoveable, yet still in excellent condition.

Three-year-old Jabe ran around, grinning all the time, charming everyone. Mary started high school at my old alma mater. Joy was still a little girl in grade school, but she was also her Grandpa Barker's undisputed favorite, which was probably good, because she needed to feel special sometimes. Johnny was in the fourth grade at school but right at home on the farm.

I was sitting at the kithen table one evening trying to work out an itinerary while Marilee and the girls were doing the dishes. We would be speaking in more than a dozen states, and I needed to work out some logical travel plans.

"Just what is your schedule for this year, Jared?" Dad asked.

"Well, first we want to give our kids a chance to get to know their grandparents, aunts and uncles, and cousins. It's good that Marilee's family is not far away so they can be with the Robison relatives also.

"Then we want to visit some of my old classmates who have been so faithful in supporting us over the years. They are a remarkable bunch, because often there just wasn't time for writing reports home, yet they sent their gifts regularly. We have to go see the Spares.

Richard and Neva Jean have a whole new crop of kids since we last saw them."

"How many do they have now?"

"Eight. Including a set of twins. Seven boys and one girl."

"There's lots of work to do on that farm," Dad declared with a knowing nod of his head.

"I'm sure there is, but you know, whenever I need a part, or something I couldn't get in the Philippines, all I have to do is mention it, and Richard takes time to find it and mail it to me. I just couldn't tell you how many times he's done that, or how much it has meant to the work.

"There are others we want to see too. While we're in the States we'd like to get some of them together to establish a board here on the homefront to handle financial receipts and maybe do some recruiting and raising of funds for special projects.

"We also want to visit the churches that have been helping us. We have lots of slides to show, demonstrating what has been accomplished through their offerings. I want them to realize that they are as much a part of this ministry as we are. We are just their representatives over there.

"I'd also like to raise enough money to get some of the equipment we need so badly."

"Oh? What all do you need?"

"Everything! When we left last time people were wanting to give us things, and we didn't know what was needed, but we do now. School equipment. Transportation."

"Transportation? I thought you wrote about buying a Jeep from one of the Wycliffe people."

"Oh, we did. For a while we had two, but they were both breaking down all the time. Vehicles deteriorate fast on those roads. We finally combined the two old Jeeps into one. It doesn't look like much, but it runs. What we really need is a truck, a cargo truck to haul lime."

"Lime? Are your folks starting to use the lime?" he asked, his interest in the subject very evident. "It would really help them. No use putting an acid-based fertilizer on an acid soil without neutralizing it first with lime."

"Ah, yeah, I know, Dad. But it's been difficult convincing the farmers of that. The bigger farmers understand, and they are using it, but reaching the small farmer has been slow."

"But they're the very ones who need it most."

"Yes, but it takes time to convince them. We've been teaching the students, and a new generation is going to grow up that understands better farming methods, but things take time in the tropics, Dad.

"We need that truck to increase our deliveries. We have the only lime in our part of the island, and right now if more farmers wanted to use it, we couldn't get it to them."

"Humph," he snorted. "We'll have to do something about that."

I was thrilled to see how much his attitude had changed. He still didn't seem to understand the importance of the spiritual work we were doing, but at least he could see we were meeting practical needs and was interested in helping us.

"What else do you really need?" he demanded.

"Well, there is something we've been praying about," I told him hesitantly. "We really need a home."

"A home? What about that little house you've been living in?"

"Well, they needed that for classrooms, and we've been living in one of the apartments over the shop for the past year. That apartment, well, let's just say it leaves a lot to be desired. It is so hot. And there's the noise and the fumes from the shop below. I think part of the reason little Jabe has been sick so much is living up there. To go to the bathroom you have to go down the stairs and through the shop to get to a deal with water on the top. We catch rainwater for showers. It's a real inconvenience. Besides they need those rooms for vocational training classes."

"How much would it cost for a decent house?"

"Well, there's a lot available across the road from the back of the campus. We could buy the lot and put up a house for about three thousand dollars."

"What kind of a house could you build for that?" he asked skeptically.

"Not one that would last as long as this one," I conceded, "but it would be adequate. More than adequate. It would seem palatial to us."

"Three thousand dollars," he mused. "It certainly seems as if your supporters would want to provide that for you."

And they did! It was just miraculous to us the response we received during that furlough. By year's end we had a big 1966 Chevrolet cargo truck with hydraulic dump bed. It was considered a 2-1/2 ton truck, but I knew that in the Philippines we'd be hauling eight or nine tons in it. We also had two pianos, a refrigerator and stove, and school equipment by the ton.

Dad seemed as thrilled as we were. He really got involved. He helped buy equipment. He helped with the packing and crating. He contacted a contractor who had a big front-end loader, and he came and picked up the crates and put them on the truck for us. It was so good to have Dad really with me.

Then a fellow named Floyd Goodwin volunteered his time to drive the truck to the coast where it would be put aboard a Navy ship bound for Subic Bay. Floyd wanted to come as a missionary but couldn't because of his health, so he helped us with the packing and drove the truck. He's just one example of so many people who have had a part in the ministry of PEEI. I consider them all unsung heros.

One of Marilee's cousins, Chaplain James Robinson, had made arrangements with the Navy to ship our gear on the USS Constellation, the biggest aircraft carrier of the day. This saved us freight charges that would have been more than twice what it would cost us to build our house.

The time for saying good-byes had come too quickly, yet we were all anxious to return to the Philippines. With all the new provisions, it almost seemed as if we were taking the States back with us.

We returned to Marbel full of expectations. Not only were we bringing back all sorts of new equipment, but an addition to the family was also making itself evident. We had had two children born in the States, both girls, and two born in the Philippines, both boys. Now we were wondering about this addition, which had been "Made in USA" and would be delivered in the Philippines.

It was good to be back "home," to be with the dear people we had come to love during our years with them. One big disappointment awaited us. While we were gone the apartment we had been living in had been turned into the library. That meant the only available space for the six of us was the three tiny rooms the Gottiers had used. We were still living over the shop, but in half the space.

I couldn't even think about beginning our house until I made sure all the work was running smoothly. Enrollment in all the schools had continued to increase, which was encouraging, but the biggest thrill came at Lake Sebu. There were sixty-five T'Bolis enrolled for this year, and they no longer ran away when big, white Americanos came to visit. Instead they ran to greet us—in English, no less. They were clean, neatly dressed, and smiling.

There was a great deal of excitement when the new truck arrived bearing all the crates of equipment. It made me wish the people who had provided all these supplies could see the reaction of our staff and students, how the equipment would be used, but most of all to realize how it encouraged our people to know there were other Christians who cared.

On the surface everything seemed to be going fine, but I had not yet discovered the conflict that was growing on the campus of King's Institute. The political problems in the area were about the same. Boy was still making life miserable for many people, but he hadn't bothered our schools while we were gone. We were still living in a frontier territory.

On September 16 Marilee received the shocking news that her brother, James Leroy Robison, had died suddenly of a heart attack. He was only forty, and he and his lovely wife, Polly, had seen us off at the airport in Seattle when we returned to the field. He had been in apparent fine health at the time.

The fact that he had died on August 20, and we hadn't heard until what would have been his birthday nearly a month later emphasized the distance between us and our relatives. The Robison family set up a memorial fund that was used to further our work in the Philippines since Jim had been so interested in the progress we were making.

When our third son was born three months later he was promptly named James Leroy.

Our three school-aged children so enjoyed helping spoil their chubby little brother during Christmas vacation they didn't want to return to Manila. Mary Beth was having trouble adjusting after having spent a year in an American high school, so we finally decided to try the correspondence course from the University of Nebraska. This was so successful that we soon had all three of them taking correspondence and living at home.

This gave Johnny an opportunity to return to his job as generator operator at the radio station. This was a very important position he had first taken on when he was only eight years old. Each morning the station went on the air at 4:00 A.M., and his regular job was to have the generator running at just the right number of cycles when the signal came to throw the switch.

DXKI was on a crossed system because they plugged into Marbel Electric when it was running. That meant Johnny had to be sure those switches were all turned off before starting up the generator, or he would blow both systems. He took this responsibility very seriously and proved himself to be very dependable.

The generator was really a blessing because the local electric service was quite undependable. So we were understandably concerned when we got a letter from the Wycliffe base saying they needed to sell the generator to raise money to buy a tractor. I wrote back and asked what kind of a tractor they needed. "Just something to use to mow the grass on the compound," they replied.

"We have several little Mustang tractors," I wrote back. "They have gasoline engines and could be used to pull a rotary mower."

The deal was made. We became the proud owners of the generator that had proved to be a necessity, and they got a tractor and a mower. Everyone was pleased the way the Lord supplied the needs of both groups.

That March we participated in the Koronadal Crusade for Christ. This was the first evangelistic campaign in our town with all the evangelical churches and mission groups cooperating. There were many decisions, and it was a good meeting all around, but we had a rather disturbing experience with one of the Filipino evangelists.

As always we opened our apartment to anyone needing a place to stay, and we were honored to have as our guest a famous evangelist.

He was sitting at our dinner table, and Marilee was serving him when he asked, "Why in the world do you folks live in a place like this?"

Marilee and I just looked at each other. How could you answer such a question? Our dwelling place was very humble with its rough sawn floors and walls, but it was what the Lord had provided for us for the time being, and it was neat and clean.

"Why do you live like this?" he repeated. "Mr. Sycip has lots of money, and your schools must be earning a profit. Why would you live in a place like this?"

I felt this was a rather insulting response to our hospitality but didn't feel I should try to explain all the circumstances.

Marilee handled it perfectly. She just smiled and replied, "This is our home."

I pulled into the Kalawag campus early one morning and was soon surrounded by students and faculty, all giving me the same message. "Boy Eglesias has been killed! He was murdered!"

After I calmed them down, the story I got was that Boy had gone to a wedding with some friends and was shot down on the highway. There was a good deal of speculation about who had shot him, but they agreed there were thirty bullet holes in him, one for every murder he was supposed to have committed.

No one was ever arrested for the crime. I think that if the killers had been found they would have received medals instead of a sentence. The whole community seemed to breathe a sigh of relief that they would no longer be terrorized by Boy and his gang. I still couldn't help but feel a bit sad. I only wish we could have reached him for Christ.

It was a year before I found time to begin building our house. Then my first priority became filling in the lot and preparing it for the building.

There seemed to be a spiritual lessson in this project. I realized we needed a firm foundation, not just the added soil we brought in; we wanted Christ to be our foundation. I thought of the verse in Ecclesiastes that talked of a "time to build." For the Barkers that time had arrived.

The plans for our house were all laid out—in my mind. I never did get around to putting them all down on paper, but Marilee had great confidence in me, and the idea of having 1500 square feet of living space seemed so miraculous to her she didn't much care how I built it.

After filling in the swampy spots I began by pouring a cement slab in four sections. Then I built concrete poles to stand on the footings. The poles were to support the house.

My idea was to have the living quarters upstairs and use the downstairs for storage, laundry, car port, tool shop, and a breezeway that could be used for recreation or just as a cool place to catch an afternoon's nap if the opportunity ever presented itself. Upstairs would be three bedrooms, bath, kitchen, office, and a large living and dining area.

Johnny was a great errand boy during the construction. That little kid could really work. I was proud of him. He'd haul buckets of water from the campus—buckets and buckets—and never complain. He was determined to help build our house.

Mary Beth was chief baby-sitter. She lined up all the little kids in the neighborhood and taught them English. She made them all play follow the leader, and when they would run, they'd have to say, "Run, run, run," or, "March, march, march," or, "Climb, climb, climb." They all learned their colors and how to count, and as a reward they were permitted rides on Star. We felt certain she would make a great teacher some day.

Joy was her mother's helper. She preferred to be indoors doing housework. She liked to help cook and was getting quite adept at making candy. Doing dishes was another matter. None of them liked that, but Joy assured us that "when we get in the new house" she was going to help us keep it shined and polished.

Jabe mostly just ran around being a boy. He was always into something. He could be the very picture of innocence with an angelic smile and dirt from head to toe. Marilee couldn't wait to move away from the shop, for she was certain that once he was removed from so much temptation he wouldn't be into so much mischief. James Leroy was a roly-poly butterball who kept the whole family smiling because he was so good-natured..

The family's excitement grew as the walls and roof went up. The roof had a large overhang so the sides would be open to allow any stray breeze to enter. As soon as it was closed in we were all ready to move. It didn't matter that there weren't any partitions, or bannisters, or doors. Minor inconveniences. We started hauling our possessions over. The braces weren't all in, and the whole house shook when anyone walked, but it was ours. The first night we camped out in our new home was December 22, 1967, which meant we awoke on our eighteenth wedding anniversary in our own home.

We got a branch of some kind of a tree and wrapped it with white paper. The kids made some stars of colored paper, and we were ready to celebrate Christmas. There was still much finishing work to be done on the house, yet we all agreed it was the best Christmas present ever. We had room to spread out a bit. But, best of all, we had the assurance the Lord in His graciousness had provided us with a home.

8
Patience

One of the most difficult things for me to learn over the years, and I'm still working on it, is patience. This is especially true when it comes to seeing needs that just must be met immediately, but for one reason or another the time is not right.

A prime example is the Monobo tribe. We were first made aware of this wild mountain tribe by some of the Wycliffe translators. They had a family living with them, working on translating the New Testament into their language. When the translation was finished they would be moving on, leaving behind God's Word in the vernacular and a band of new believers. There was a great need for a permanent work that could establish churches and schools.

I had taken the family up to Lake Sebu for one of the annual camps and then returned to the valley to carry on with the work at one of the farm projects. One of the Wycliffe pilots, Paul Carlson, had offered to pick me up at the airport near Kalawag and fly me back up to Lake Sebu, if I didn't mind a side trip into Manobo territory. How could I refuse an offer like that?

"I've been making two or three trips a day in there," Paul told me. "They are having all kinds of difficulties. Right now they have a good rice crop but can't get it out to market it, so I've been hauling in supplies they need and carrying out the rice to a place where they can get a decent price.

"A bit of a sticky situation developed yesterday, though," he confided.

"What's that?"

"Well, one of the Lymans' kids flew in with me. A little guy, maybe nine years old. He'd grown up back in there and wanted to go along for a visit. His folks said OK, so I took him along. We landed, unloaded, and then loaded up the rice, and he was going to stay until I came with the next load. Problem is, a heavy rain developed and I couldn't get back to pick him up. He's still up there. Spent the night there by himself, and his parents are pretty worried about him. A little kid by himself. No way of contacting him to find where he is or with whom."

I could readily understand the parents' concern, so I jumped aboard the little Helio Courier and we took off at once. As we touched down on the landing strip I could see all these dark, long-haired, wild-looking mountain people lined up along the side of the runway, with one blond little kid jumping up and down in their midst.

As we came to a stop, he came running up just as happy as he could be. "Look what I've got! Look what I've got!" he shouted. We climbed down and inspected the contents of a big powdered milk carton he was holding. It was full of bats. "We went bat hunting!" he exclaimed. "With bows and arrows."

The pilot radioed back to the Wycliffe base to assure the Lymans that their son was not only all right but had been well cared for and was having a ball. The bats he had were the local variety of fruit bats. They have about a three-foot wing span and, since they eat only fruit, are good for eating. Or so I'd been told.

While the pilot made another trip, I hiked into the little barrio there on the mountain just to look around. I discovered a few settlers from the lowlands. It was amazing to me that they had settlers in a place as remote as that, but that gave me someone I could talk with.

It was obvious the people were quite desperate. They were so thin. Many were sick. The most impressive illness was the massive goiters that you never saw among the valley people, who ate lots of fish. There was no school in the whole area, and everyone I talked to seemed most eager to have one.

The spiritual, medical, and physical needs, as well as the need for education, was so overwhelming that I wanted to promise I'd be back. That I'd bring help. But I couldn't. We were still struggling to provide teachers and workers for the projects we already had going. There was no way I could obligate PEEI to do anything for these people, but in the back of my head I thought, *Someday. Someday.*

We flew on toward Lake Sebu, but a menacing-looking rain shower prevented us from landing there. "Let's go to Sinalong," Paul suggested. "We'll get Vivian Forsberg or Lillian Underwood to make us some ice cream." So we flew to the other end of the T'Boli territory to spend the night.

We still had the Lyman boy and his bats with us, so the Wycliffe gals got some of the T'Bolis to clean them for us and they made bat *adobo*. Now *adobo* is good eating. Filipinos usually make it with cubes of pork or chicken. They marinate the meat in a sauce with lots of garlic, then simmer it until tender and serve it over rice.

I'd always heard that fruit bats were good to eat, but somehow I felt very hesitant about taking the first bite. The second was no problem at all. It was delicious! Rather like chicken, but sweeter. When we left for Lake Sebu the next morning Lillian sent along some of the *adobo* for Marilee to try. "Just don't tell her what it is until after she's tasted it," she insisted.

I shared the *adobo* with my wife and also my concern for the Manobo. "But there is just no way we could begin a work for them without a plane."

"What about the Wycliffe planes?"

"Well, they have been very generous in allowing us to fly their planes when our plans fit their schedules, but we couldn't depend on them to fly us all the time. They're overworked as it is. Also, as the New Testament translations are completed in southern Mindanao, they will be flying less and less in our vicinity. The only solution would be to have a plane of our own."

"That seems impossible."

"Yeah, I know. But who knows? Maybe Johnny really will become a pilot when he grows up. If we have a pilot, surely the Lord will provide a plane."

"But that will be years from now."

"Right. Waiting can be very difficult when you see the people in such need. For now, I guess we'll just have to pray the Lord will grant us patience."

Impatience is such a weakness of mine that I have to stop and marvel at how much patience our supporters have had with me. After ten years on the field we finally got around to producing our first brochure. Even this was just a 9-by-11-inch page that folded over into a small leaflet, but it had a bit of the history of PEEI, some pictures, and a challenge to help us meet the many opportunities for service and witness in Mindanao.

In an age where advertising has become something of an art form, it is surprising how little publicity our mission has had. My excuse is I've just been too busy working at the task to take time to tell people what is going on. One thing is certain, our work has endured and grown over the years not because of the clever campaigns of some public relations firm but through the power of the Holy Spirit.

I'm not saying that it's wrong to advertise what the Lord is doing, only that this work has grown in spite of the lack of publicity. One of the biggest factors that has made this true is the faithfulness of folks in the homeland who have supported us over the years even though our prayer letters sometimes could more accurately be called our Annual Report.

After ten years we were beginning to have some homegrown laborers to help in the work. If I stop and think of all those in whom we have invested time, money, patience, and prayers who have gone off to pursue their own goals, I get discouraged. Their lives have been enriched by the education provided because of the support of PEEI, but they have never come back to say, "Thank you," and, "How can we help?"

Those who have become involved are real gems. I guess the percentage is about one in ten. Come to think of it, that is the same percentage the Lord had when He healed the ten lepers, so I guess it's biblical. I wish I could tell about all of our graduates who are now devoting their lives to the Lord's work, but since I can't, let me give a few examples.

William Layda, the young lad who made a profession of faith on my first survey trip to Mindanao, by 1968 had finished Bible school and was serving with Overseas Missionary Fellowship in Indonesia. He not only became a great example for our students, but he also stretched our own vision as we realized how much more acceptable the ministry of a Filipino was in another, so-called third-world country, than that of an American. With his background of local languages, it was much easier for him to become fluent in Indonesian than it would have been for a monolingual American. Also, he fit in physically and was better able to adapt to local customs.

After receiving one of his prayer letters telling of the danger as well as the challenge of his work, Marilee waxed eloquent. "I'm going to make a prophecy," she declared. "Someday the Lord is going to raise up Christian Filipinos to bring revival to mainland China! And by helping train these young people, we are having a real part in preparing for that event." My wife can get a bit carried away with her enthusiasm at times, but I have to admit that possibility is exciting to contemplate.

Closer to home, when we needed a new announcer at DXKI we hired Alvaro Estabillo, one of our students. Alvaro had been one of our first high school students at King's and was now in the college.

"When did you become a Christian?" I asked him during the job interview.

"When I was in second year high school. I became involved in an incident here in school due to my rebelliousness," he answered, looking rather embarrassed. "I had drawn a picture of a man with horns and a big tummy, and I named it 'Mr. Mojica,' my character education teacher. I got caught, and he took me to the principal, Mr. Llobrera. Instead of punishing me, he dealt with me from the Scriptures, and I prayed there in his classroom to receive Christ."

We gave him a trial, and he did extremely well—announcing in English and Tagalog, doing the news, education programs, and the dedications on our deejay program. When he was sick one day his girl friend, Ninfa Villanueva, took over for him and did such a good job we hired them both. There was one rather unusual thing about their relationship. He is Ilocano and she is Ilongo. During those days there sometimes was trouble between those two groups. If there was a fight, the tribes would group together, so it was interesting to see how a common Christian commitment could overcome such difficulties.

Another example of this is Badawi, our first Moslem convert. We had sent him to Manila to Bible school, but his stomach refused to accept the food they served. The rich greasy food made him sickly, so he had to come back to Mindanao.

After finishing college at King's he taught for us at Lake Sebu and worked on the farm. We had an unusually good relationship with his family, and his father told me more than once, "Badawi is your son." His parents couldn't go against his new faith when they saw the results.

Magdalena Maglunob, Mags, had now finished her education on the "Go Now Pay Later" plan, as had Sonie Larano, another of our promising students. They both kept their agreement to repay us, and it wasn't easy for either of them because of family responsibilities.

Once in a while if I get really discouraged about how many we are reaching, the Lord sends someone along to remind me that this is His work, and it isn't really important whether I always know what becomes of those we try to win. I was over at Central Philippine

University in Ilo-Ilo City looking for new teachers when a good-looking, well-dressed fellow came up to me in the library. He gave me a big smile and said, "You ought to know me."

At first I drew a complete blank. Then I got a mental image of an irate young farm worker standing up in the middle of our very first Bible conference and yelling, "I came here to kill someone!"

"Carabao!" I exclaimed. He looked so different I could hardly believe my eyes.

"I was 'Carabao,'" he responded. "Now I follow the Lord. I want to ask forgiveness for the aggravation I caused you. I'm a Christian now, and I've come to college here to prepare myself for service."

As we talked a bit he told me that the Lord had first started dealing with him back at that Bible conference. I hadn't seen him in the ten years since, and our paths haven't crossed again. It seems every time I begin to lose patience with some "impossible" person, the Lord reminds me that His Word does not return to Him void. It is very difficult to be patient at times, but it is worth it.

When it comes to telling stories about having my patience tried, I think I could write a whole book about some of the equipment we've had to use over the years. We've used stuff that would have been relegated to the junk pile back in the States. It takes lots of ingenuity to utilize equipment that has really had it, especially when parts are next to impossible to obtain. I've had to improvise and cannibalize almost every mechanical implement we have.

Take the old weapons carrier, for example. This big four-wheel-drive Army vehicle first belonged to the Weavers. Pop got it as World War II surplus. It used so much gas I think even the Army was glad to get rid of the thing.

The Weavers used this heavy, lumbering old vehicle for transporting goods up the mountain to their sari-sari store in Lake Sebu. With its big tires and heavy springs, the ruggedly built truck could pull the steep mountain grades. It came equipped with a winch and cable to pull itself out of mudholes.

In those days I was hiking up to Lake Sebu on a regular monthly schedule to take the teachers their salaries and check on how everything was going. I'd climb up one day, stay a day, and come down the next. There were times I would pass Pop's wife going up in the weapons carrier, and then when I'd come down two days later, she would still be on the way up.

The weapons carrier wouldn't have been so slow if the road had been better. I don't know if I should even use the word *road*. Back in Kansas it would probably have been classified as a cow path. It certainly would never have been dignified with a name or number. Farm animals that traveled the path left a track every time they stepped in a wet place. Rain water would stand in that track, making it deeper. The next animal that came through would make it deeper still. The mud is actually two feet deep in many of those places, and the small mountain ponies can hardly make it through.

When the old Army truck came along, it would sink in the ooze, and the driver would have to tie the cable to a tree, and the truck would pull itself through the hole. Of course, the bumper would scoop out a good deal of mud on its way through, so the hole would get deeper and deeper.

Since there aren't enough large trees in the correct spots along the way, it was standard practice to carry along an old axle and a large hammer. When there weren't any trees to tie the cable to, they'd pound the yard-long axle into the ground and tie up to that.

Whenever Mary Weaver and her driver made a trip up with supplies, she would load the carrier with cases of Coke, cartons of groceries, drums of gasoline and kerosene, and boxes of assorted paraphernalia until it seemed impossible to drive that overloaded vehicle up the mountain. Maybe that's why it took so long. The heavier the load, the deeper the mud holes would become when they pulled through them. In the flat sections on top of the mountain I've seen holes so deep you could walk straight across on top of the truck. They'd get stuck in one of those holes, and the engine would drown out. Then mud and water would get into all their supplies and make the biggest mess.

With that in mind you can understand how enthusiastic I was when I first heard that Pop wanted to sell the weapons carrier. He had decided to get out of storekeeping and was going to live in the valley for a while. Pop had a restless spirit and was always changing his mind about what he wanted to do or where he wanted to live. The only thing he seemed certain about was that he didn't want to return to the States. From what he read in newspapers and magazines everything had changed so, it didn't seem like home to him any longer.

"Now that they've built that bridge across the Allah River, you ought to have a truck to go up the mountain, Jerry," he mentioned casually one evening after filling up on Marilee's upsidedown pineapple cake. "Save you all that hiking up and down."

"I'm not sure the honor would be worth the effort," I replied, leaning back in my recliner.

"But the more the school grows, the more equipment you have

to carry up there. And your camps are a big success, but then you wouldn't have to ferry all those students back and forth on the boats," he continued.

I let him go on convincing me for a while, just to give him a hard time. I'd already decided to try to trade off one of our jeeps for the big truck, for just the reasons he'd mentioned. Besides, I'd helped him maintain the truck and was probably the only one who knew how to keep the thing running.

"That Bailey bridge is really something," I said, changing the subject. "I'll bet the US Corps of Engineers never realized when they first constructed those bridges with their interchangeable panels up in Manila that they would be used over and over. Why I bet some of those—"

"Jerry," he interrupted. "What I need is a jeep now that I'm living in Surallah."

"OK, Pop," I conceded. "Let's make a deal."

We made the deal, and PEEI became the owner of a weapons carrier. As the chief driver, I'd have to supply my own patience.

For some reason it is always hardest to have patience with your own family. I think Marilee should be granted an honorary doctorate in patience for the time she has devoted to getting kids through school by correspondence. The girls had a hard time with their high school courses, partly because they never wanted to miss the activities at King's, or the youth group, or the "Challenge to Youth" radio broadcast, or the latest wedding, and so on. They were always busy and didn't lack for friends, just time for studies.

John had the hardest time. I'd listen in while he and Marilee were studying modern math together. Sometimes I didn't know who was the teacher and who was the student, but they were both far ahead of me, so I kept quiet. Keeping at his studies was quite a task.

Jabe seemed more suited to the discipline of home study and was doing well. He also excelled in being a big brother to little Jimmy, who was learning to talk to his family in English and his friends in Ilongo.

The boys were all Filipino in disposition as well as by birth. I kept them busy working on the farm and learning mechanical skills. As the girls grew older, it was more difficult for them to be living on a mission field. One of the big bones of contention was clothes—or the lack thereof.

"Mom, the Filipinas are better dressed than we are!" they would wail. Marilee would drag out the latest missionary barrel and say, "Well, let's see what fits."

"Oh,no!"

"Not again."

"Come on, girls. Some of these things are nice. Now, Mary you try this blue dress on, and Joy, this yellow one looks as if it will fit you."

"Can't we ever have anything new?" Joy wailed.

"Well, girls, it seems to me that you need some kind of a project so you can earn spending money," I interjected. I'd been raised on the good ol' Protestant work ethic, and I still believed hard work never hurt anyone. If my girls wanted money, they'd have to earn it.

"But what can we do?" Mary asked. "It isn't like the States where you can baby-sit or something. There are no jobs available for us."

"Oh, you can always find some way of earning money if you want to badly enough. I was over at the Dole plantation a couple of weeks ago and noticed they had started a poultry project. If you want, I could ask Mr. John to bring us down a batch of chicks, you could raise them, slaughter them, and sell them. I feel certain there would be a ready market for them, but you'd have to do the work."

"We will! We will!" they promised in chorus.

I wondered if their enthusiasm would last when they had to clean out the chicken coops and cut off the chickens' heads and gut them, but we ordered 100 broiler chicks sent down by plane from Manila as a trial. The kids pitched in and did a good job with the chickens, and the eight weeks it took the chicks to reach maturity went very quickly.

On the eighth Saturday we set up a production line to prepare the chickens for sale. We hired a couple of the students to help. I cut off most of the heads that first time, then handed them to Joy, who hung them by their feet to bleed. Next they were dipped into a pot of boiling water, then handed on to the pluckers. Mary, our biologist, cut out the innards, and handed them on to be bagged.

We had the 100 chickens ready for sale before noon, and the customers had lined up waiting for the fresh meat. Word of mouth really works in our little village, and the word had spread. Our project was so successful that the girls decided to try it again. This grew into a regular poultry business, and before we knew it, there were 2,000 chickens clucking away in our back yard. We butchered about 200 a week and had an outlet at the marketplace.

What had started out as a little family project had grown to such proportions that it had almost become a full-time job, and some of our students were working their way through college in the poultry business. Our girls were delighted with the results of their labors, although I've heard Mary say, "The rest of my life, I'll never be able to stand the smell of raw chicken."

The time had come to make arrangements to turn the project over to King's so they could use it in teaching animal husbandry. This would benefit the school and the students, but the main reason we had to let it go was that our girls were returning to the States to complete their educations.

Letting them go wasn't easy. This was a decision we had put off as long as possible. Mary Beth was eighteen and Joy sixteen. We'd kept them with us as long as we felt we could. Mary lacked only a few high school courses and wanted to enter nursing school after graduation. Because of the difficulties they had had with taking high school by correspondence, we felt it best for Joy to take her last two years of high school in the States.

It was a great comfort to know our loved ones in the States would give them loving homes while they were separated from us, but it was still hard to say good-bye. Marilee went with them to Manila to see them safely on the plane with a missionary group flight, and we knew my sisters would be there to meet them in Seattle.

Marilee returned by herself. She looked so forlorn when she got off that plane.

"We started off our missionary careers with two little girls, but now we are on the field with three sons," I reminded her.

"But John will be going to Nasuli to the Wycliffe school soon," she replied. "I'll just have my two little boys at home."

I thought she had gone to sleep that night, but the bed started quivering, and I knew she was crying. "What is it, honey?" I asked. "The girls will be all right. They are really quite mature for their ages, and besides, you know we can trust the Lord to protect them."

"I know." She sniffled. "It's not that. I just wonder—I'm afraid—that they don't know how much I love them." Then she really started blubbering. "I just wish they knew how hard it was for me to see them go. Having them go so very far away isn't easy, even if it is for their good."

I'm not much of a comforter. I just cried along with her. It did seem they had grown up too quickly.

A few days later a little package came in the mail addressed to me.

It was from the girls and contained a letter explaining the contents. "We took our spending money and bought this for you to give to Mom on your anniversary. We wanted it to be sort of a symbol of our family's love for one another."

I opened the box. It held a blue star sapphire ring in a gold setting. I knew that even in Hong Kong it must have cost them every cent they had. It was indeed a beautiful symbol, and I knew how very precious it would be to Marilee. I couldn't help but think that it takes a lot of patience to raise children, but they're worth it.

9
Accepting What I Can't Understand

The political situation in Mindanao was becoming increasingly stressful, so John Sycip made a special effort to be here to vote in November of 1969. The province of Cotabato was to be divided into four provinces with our hometown of Koronadal as the capital of the new province of South Cotabato. This made our location even more strategic, for it was becoming a boom town. Because of his great love for this place, John kept his voting residence here.

He was his usual cheerful self, spreading goodwill wherever he went. When he left he asked if there was anything we needed our "messenger boy" to bring the next time. He was always calling himself a "glorified messenger boy," and would never take seriously his title as president of PEEI.

When we heard he had gone into the hospital for a checkup, we weren't particularly concerned. He had seemed so healthy on his last visit. Then word came that they had discovered cancer in his lung. Long months of confinement were difficult for such an active man to bear, yet he took comfort in knowing many people were praying for him. When he was released from the hospital in March his myriad friends rejoiced.

Soon he was back in his office, and I visited him there. It was business as usual—phones ringing, people rushing in and out. As I

waited for an opportunity to talk with him I recalled an event he
had shared with me when I first knew him.

"My father was born in the Philippines," he had told me, "so we
were all natural citizens. When the Japanese invaded our country in
World War II, my father was blacklisted because he had been very
active in the Chinese community. Our entire extended family, about
forty of us, evacuated to an island north of Luzon, not far from
Taiwan.

"It was just a small island, and we had to live in nipa houses, but
there was food enough and no Japanese. We remained in hiding
there until after Manila was liberated. The Americans did not control
all the islands yet, but the capital was free. One morning shortly after
we had heard the news on our radio, some natives approached us
and said, 'The Americans are here!' We were so happy and excited.

"Then the American planes came, and they strafed us and bombed
us. They killed fourteen of our family. One brother, a sister, an uncle,
an aunt, my grandmother, and some children. My wife was carrying
our baby in her arms when she was killed.

"Later we asked the Americans why they attacked us, and they
said that from the air they could not distinguish us from Japanese.
They were very sorry. It had all been a mistake. They returned us
to Manila where they restored to us the property the Japanese had
confiscated from us.

"The Lord was very good to me and later gave me another fine
wife and three more children, Ady, Jimmy, and Grace. My Navidad
loves all my children the same and is as good a mother to the older
children as to the young ones."

Sitting in his office, watching him dealing with some American
businessmen, I could detect no bitterness whatsoever. There seemed
to be no hatred or animosity in this exceptional Christian gentleman.
He had been a blessing to my life, to my family, and to the many
people connected with the Philippine Evangelical Enterprises. I felt
an overwhelming gratitude that the Lord had seen fit to spare his
life that he might continue to be a witness for Him.

A few weeks later he was back in the hospital. As soon as I could
arrange it, I made another trip to Manila and visited him. He was
deeply sedated and couldn't talk with me. His family was gathered
around him, deeply upset at seeing him in such pain. I couldn't
understand why the Lord allowed this. John was such a good man,
a faithful witness devoted to extending the Word not only through
PEEI, but also through FEBC and the Gideons, as well as Grace

Church and Grace Christian School, which he had helped found in Manila. I couldn't understand it, but I had to accept it.

Just a few days after I returned to Mindanao word came that he had died. I was glad he had been released from his pain and thankful for the assurance that we would one day meet again.

Marilee and I went to the funeral. It was a beautiful testimony of the influence of one man who had tried to serve his Lord in such a humble manner. Thousands of people came to pay their respects in the largest funeral service I'd ever seen. Well-dressed people drove up in chauffered automobiles, and very humble people walked to the church. It was a fitting farewell for one of God's choicest "messenger boys."

Real trouble was brewing at Lake Sebu. The elementary school began the year with an enrollment of 110, which was quite encouraging. The problems were coming from outsiders. With the coming of the "road," more and more lowland people were pushing in to get the land that had traditionally belonged to the T'Boli. With a continual feeling of unrest it was inevitable that there would come an outbreak of violence.

Shortly after the beginning of the new decade some lowlanders abused one of the T'Bolis. Following the revenge system, one of the outlanders was killed shortly after. Then the other side had to retaliate. This continued until three or four had been killed on each side, and the T'Bolis were living in fear. Many of them evacuated, and soon the school was almost without pupils.

When the T'Bolis would ask me why such a thing should come upon their little settlement, I was hard put to answer, especially when those killed were innocent of any wrongdoing. I only know there is evil in this world, and until the Lord Jesus returns there are going to be happenings that we can't understand. Accepting them, turning them over to the Lord, and going on in faith believing that some day He will make all things right, is about all we can do. Without a plane there was no way we could have quick access to the situation and not much we could do to protect our teachers except pray.

We had mowed a field near King's to be used as an air strip as a matter of faith as much as anything else. The first time it worked out for Johnny to fly home from school in Nasuli with one of the Wycliffe pilots, he was really impressed. He had been flying in commercial planes as long as he could remember, but that was nothing to the thrill of his first flight in one of the little single-engine Helios.

The need for a plane was reemphasized later when Marilee had a severe abcess and had to be transported to Davao City for surgery at Brokenshire Hospital. It would have been a much quicker, easier trip by plane. While I was there visiting her I had a checkup myself and, after some laboratory work, was informed I had a bit of a problem.

"You've become infected with schistosomiasis," the doctor informed me.

"What?"

"Snail fever," he explained. "It's endemic in your area. It is a parasitic disease due to infestation with blood flukes, a parasitic worm that inhabits snails in the rivers in Allah valley."

"I probably got it in the irrigation system at Kalawag," I ventured. "You can't do work like that without getting wet."

"Well, we'll start you on a course of treatment."

I figured I'd start treatment after we got Marilee out of the hospital. She was doing fine, as a matter of fact. No patient ever had more loving, tender care than she received. Two of her nurses were graduates of our high schools. Meeting former students like those fine young women is one of the joys and rewards of our service.

We got back home, and I started on the medicine the doctor had prescribed. I believe that stuff is strong enough to kill the bugs! It nearly killed me. It has arsenic in it. I got weaker and weaker. I was finally to the point where I could hardly move. I couldn't cut my own meat, and then I couldn't use my elbows enough to bring the food to my mouth.

"I'm stopping this medicine," I finally declared. "I'd rather die of snail fever than arsenic poisoning."

"But you can't do that," Marilee insisted. "The worms will lay eggs in your heart or your brain, just any part of your body. You've got to get rid of them."

I still refused to take more of the medicine. It was ruining my health. So I just quit, never did go back to the doctor, and I still don't know just what kind of bug I'm carrying around. I do know I never completely regained my strength after taking that medicine.

I didn't have time to be sick. There were too many other things to fill my time. The unrest at Lake Sebu was but an indication of the problems the whole country was facing. These were decisive days in the Islands, for conditions were changing dramatically. I didn't want to alarm the folks back home, so in my letters I tried to avoid any sensationalism, but I asked for prayer. A new constitutional convention was being planned, and many of the proposed changes were vital to the future of our ministry.

It was nearly time for another furlough, and though we were hesitant to leave while there were so many problems, we were anxious to get home to see our daughters. A new couple, Jim and Barbara Hibschman, was now on the field helping us. Jim was serving as dean of the college department at King's and teaching Christian education subjects. I had complete confidence in their ability to handle things while we were gone.

When Ben Calica, a member of the FEBC who was assigned to our station, came to me with a suggestion, I wondered why I hadn't considered it before myself. "We need to have a church here," he said. "With the number of boarding students growing all the time, it is impossible to provide transportation for all of them to the services in other churches."

It was Ben's idea, so I let him go to work on it, and he became the founder of the King's Church. Because we had so many people on our staff who were qualified to preach and needed the training and experience, we did not call a pastor. This worked out amazingly well, for every member seemed to realize his responsibility toward the church.

One thing that really pleased me was that from the inception King's Church has been missions-minded. Fifty percent of their offerings go to missions. They help support the William Laydas in Indonesia and give to DXKI and Inter-Varsity, to tribal ministries and orphanages. I think it should be a challenge to Stateside churches to consider this little band of believers here on the mission field who realize their responsibility for spreading the gospel to others.

Our desire to help conflicted with our anxiety to take our furlough before the situation became more unstable. We had to wait for Johnny to finish eighth grade at Nasuli so he could begin his high school in the States. We waited—and missed both Mary's wedding and Joy's graduation from high school.

We were saddened we hadn't been able to attend those two important occasions, but we were home when Badawi came to tell us good-bye.

"I feel I need to go back and work with my people," he said softly.

Our first Moslem convert had been such a good and faithful friend, we hated to see him go. We needed him to teach at Lake Sebu, but we could understand his desire to return to his people now that they were having a mini-civil war in his home district.

"There are many rebels in your territory," I reminded him. "It could be dangerous."

"I know." He smiled sweetly, shuffled his feet, tipped his head, and looked up at me. "I need to be a witness to my own people."

We embraced in parting, and I watched him walk down the dusty path. I wondered if I would ever see him again.

We were encouraged that our furlough plans were in accordance with God's will by the return of Belen and Felipe Fernandez. Belen was the young teacher who had always been such a special friend to Mary Beth. She had first heard of our work in the Inter-Varsity Fellowship Christian group in Manila and came to Kalawag just in time for the big locust invasion. In 1967 we transferred her to King's to become my secretary, and when she and our military instructor began courting, we knew nothing about it until the engagement was announced.

Now this very capable newly married couple was returning to take on some of the responsibility at King's. Together with the Hibschmans we felt confident the work would run smoothly in our absence. I don't understand all the ways the Lord works to bring people to the place where He needs them, but I happily accept it.

That furlough we had very convenient living arrangements in Stanley, Kansas. Being reunited with our family was naturally a happy occasion, and yet that furlough was marred by the news from the Philippines. It may seem strange that the worse the political situation became, the more we wanted to be back there. Mindanao had become our home. That doesn't mean we have lost our love or allegience to our own country, but we have become so identified with our Filipino brethren that it hurt to hear of turmoil going on in our beloved adopted country.

We were extremely grateful that even though there were strikes, riots, and demonstrations going on in many of the schools throughout the country, our campuses remained peaceful. Having a student body with so many truly dedicated Christians and a faculty likewise committed made all the difference. This was a point I made over and over as I traveled around doing deputation that year.

We didn't get to see as much of Mary and our new son-in-law as we would have liked that year, but they were happy so we felt content about them. Joy came and stayed with us and helped care for the boys while Marilee and I traveled. There was one special trip that Joy and I took to LeTourneau College. She was a new driver and thrilled at the opportunity to get behind the wheel. It was really fun spending time with her, and we talked about her future.

"I'll never fall in love," she insisted. "I'm just not interested in boys. I'm going to get my education and be a missionary."

Naturally this pleased me, so I made arrangements for her to enroll in my alma mater, Kansas State. She got a scholarship, and we set aside some money for her. Having her plans all made made it easier for us to leave her.

When we reached the West Coast we had to face leaving our son for the first time. Johnny would be staying with my sister's family in Seattle and attending the Christian high school there. Doris and her husband, Jim Lombardo, just take our kids into their family and make them feel right at home.

As on previous furloughs the Lord raised up more equipment for the work. A semi-trailer load! To top that off, He sent us a couple of new recruits who were coming as short-term assistants. My sister Lillian Walker, a well-trained, experienced secretary, was coming for two years to help in the office and to set up a vocational training program in the college.

David Spare, the eldest son of our close friends from college days, was going to spend a year helping develop the agricultural program so the mission could be more self-supporting. Dave had had lots of experience on the family farm, and I knew he wasn't afraid of hard work. If we had known just how ticklish the situation was going to become in Mindanao, I wouldn't have felt so complacent about bringing out a couple of raw recruits.

While we were in transit, the "Ilaga," Ilongo for "Rats," were attacking the Moslem community. Persecution of the Moslems had been going on for years, but not this overtly. We returned home to find the campus full of Moslem evacuees. They were camping out in the dormitories, and when the class rooms emptied at night, they would sleep on the floors.

The Hibschmans were doing all they could to help them. "You've often said you'd like an opportunity to minister to the Moslems," Jim reminded me. "Now's our chance."

"Well, I was really planning on unpacking first, but. . ." I shrugged. Coming back to the field is always a little like jumping headfirst into a pool of icy water. There's never any time to adjust. You just have to come up swimming.

"We will certainly do all we can for them," I agreed more seriously. "We just have to remind the staff that the most effective witness with

a Moslem is to show that we care. If we get into religious arguments
with them, we will never accomplish anything."

As soon as they could, government officials stepped in to help out
in the situation, and the Moslems were relocated after a few weeks.
The relocation centers compounded the problem, though, because
before this time the Moslems were more or less scattered around the
area in little communities, not in any one concentrated area. Now
they were grouped together by themselves, and after so many years
of persecution it was inevitable that they should begin to organize.

In a culture where "revenge" is the unwritten law, it was only a
matter of time before someone was made to pay for the burned-out
homes, gutted villages, and innocent deaths. The Moslems formed
the Moro National Liberation Front to avenge the years of governmental neglect and mistreatment by fellow Filipinos. It was their goal
to secede from the rest of the nation and form an independent
Moslem government.

The news from Manila wasn't any more encouraging. The whole
country was in turmoil. There was a tremendous political bombing
in one of the large plazas in Manila, and several politicians lost limbs.
A huge demonstration was aimed at the presidential palace, the gates
of the surrounding wall were broken down, and the mob rushed in
as preparations were being made to fly the president to safety.

Such anarchy couldn't continue. We began praying for the Lord
to raise up someone to bring peace. Our prayers were answered in
an unexpected way. Martial law was declared.

The most frightening thing about being under martial law was
that no one knew just what to expect. Suddenly everything was under
military control. A curfew was established. Soldiers were patrolling
everywhere. There was a complete news blackout. Rumors spread
malignantly.

Even in a situation as volatile as this one, God had His man in
the right place. A Christian who had contact with the president
pleaded the case of the FEBC stations, and they were permitted to
return to the air after only forty-eight hours. DXKI came back on,
and news-hungry people all over our end of the island listened with
rapt attention for reliable news. Our permission was a very controlled
situation, and we had to abide by strict guidelines. Only official press
releases from the government news organization could be broadcast,
but people were eager to learn just what was expected of them.

We had a little shortwave radio, and occasionally we would hear something from BBC or VOA, but that was quite limited, and the news they were getting out of the country had no doubt been censored. The situation was as unsettling for us as it was for everyone else. We tried to remain calm and go about our business as circumspectly as possible. All the staff was praying we would soon be able to reopen the schools.

One of the first edicts from the new military command ordered the surrender of all firearms. At every checkpoint there were signs: SURRENDER YOUR FIREARMS, OR DIE. I had a gun. The government knew I had it, for I had been licensed to have it for the protection of the school, but I had to turn it in.

The Moslem community reacted strongly to this new law. After all the persecution they had suffered in the previous months they weren't about to give up their guns. They had lost so much while having firearms to protect themselves, they couldn't help but wonder what their fate would be if they were defenseless. "Maybe they want our firearms so they can kill us all" was a comment heard often. Another was, "You can have my wife, but not my gun!" These men would either disappear into the mountains, or they would bury their guns nearby.

One of the most upsetting problems during these days was being constantly stopped at checkpoints. I'd pull up as ordered, and the next thing I knew there would be a machine gun pointed in my direction. I realized I was probably safer as a foreigner than if I'd been a local barrio boy, but I still found it disconcerting. You could never tell what one of these cocky guys might decide to do, and often it was obvious they had been drinking.

One time we were stopped, and the soldiers had been having a drinking party. They invited me to have a drink with them, and I said, "No. I don't drink." The officer of the group got really insulted because I refused to drink with him.

"You think you are too good to drink with us?" he snarled.

"No, sir. I'm a Christian, and I don't drink alcoholic beverages."

"Well, you better drink one now!"

He was really applying the pressure when one of his subordinates came up and said, "I'll take care of this," and he led the officer away. I jumped back in the truck and got out of there.

Encounters like this at the many checkpoints proved to be the biggest hassle we had to face during the first days under martial law. Because we had schools and farms scattered throughout the area I had to travel back and forth and couldn't avoid these contacts. I learned to be very polite, not to carry extra money with me, and to allow them to "appropriate" an extra gallon or so of diesel fuel if they insisted.

My sister, Lillian, seemed to take all the pressure better than I would have expected. She worked with Belen in the office and made meticulous plans for starting a secretarial department at King's. She found some of our methods sloppy and didn't seem convinced when we told her we had found it better to do the best we could under the circumstances than to wait until everything was just perfect. It was also difficult for her to adjust to "Filipino time," that is, being late. Overall I was really proud of her, for she knew her subject well and worked hard in spite of the unusual circumstances.

After the first weeks of martial law, we overcame the fears of uncertainty and decided the total effect had been for good. President Marcos had declared that this was to be "a benevolent form of martial law," and that was proving true. With the curfew there was a marked reduction of crime and lawlessness. The country seemed remarkably peaceful.

With the civil authorities and judicial system superceded by the military, anyone who became an enemy of the army had no court of appeals. They were hauled off to a stockade and frequently not heard from again. This put a decided damper on those involved in subversive or criminal acts against the government. As law-abiding residents we had nothing to fear.

The instability of the situation seemed, remarkably, to make people more spiritually aware. Our teachers and students returned to the campus with a much more aggressive evangelistic spirit than ever before. Although we hadn't anticipated it, we accepted the fact that martial law had increased our opportunities to minister.

10
Living with Fear

As if we didn't have enough problems in Mindanao, we received a letter from Joy with some unsettling news. "I really don't like school much," she wrote. "How would you feel if I decided to become a housewife?" It seemed she and the pastor's son had discovered each other. I wired back, "CONTINUE SCHOOLING." The next letter we got, she was making her wedding plans. This from the girl who was never going to fall in love!

Marilee received a telegram from her relatives begging us to return to the States. They had heard about martial law being declared in the Island and were afraid we were in danger. We never seriously considered leaving. How could we tell our people to pray for God's protection and then leave ourselves? Besides, we didn't feel any real threat to our safety.

We were discouraged a bit when the authorities refused us permission to begin a work among the Manobos. The needy tribe had been on my heart ever since the day I ate bat *adobo,* and we had returned from furlough with the Manobos as one of our top priorities. A logging firm had opened a road of sorts back into those mountains, and we felt it was time to at least make a survey, but the officials were adamant. There were too many rebels back in there, and they were concerned for our safety.

Requirements were laid down by the "New Society" in the Philippines affecting our schools, and implementing them was taking all my time anyway. The government decided more stress should be

placed on technical and career-oriented training. We were much
better prepared and equipped to carry out these new guidelines than
most schools. Our main problem was a lack of teachers with masters
degrees in the proper fields. We'd have to help some of our teachers
upgrade their qualifications.

One of my major concerns was the safety of the three teachers
serving at the T'Boli school at Lake Sebu. Mags was now the principal
there, and having a lovely young lady like her up in the mountains
worried me. There were many soldiers stationed nearby to protect
the people from the rebels. I just wondered if our teachers might
need protection from the soldiers.

Even during these times of stress, God was at work. Pop and Mary
Weaver both accepted Christ as Savior. "It wasn't anything you said,"
Pop informed me with a twinkle in his eye. "But I've been watching
the way you live, all you Christians, and I decided what you had was
real. And I sure needed it."

It takes a long time for hardheaded people to realize that, but
when they do it's a source of joy to all the people who love them.

At Christmas time we decided to load the old weapons carrier with
presents and coconut seedlings to distribute among the T'Bolis. We
packed in used clothing, powdered milk, cooking oil, corn meal, and
other staples along with our gifts. Marilee and I were in the front
with Melly Cuenca, one of our teachers, and her young son. Jimmy,
Jabe, and Dave Spare were riding in the back with all the cargo.

The road was fairly dry but quite steep and a little rocky, so we
weren't going too fast. Because it was dry, I guess I got a bit careless
and didn't use the four-wheel-drive. When we got to a real steep
point, I had to shift into the lowest gear to keep going. For some
reason, when I shifted into low, the rear axle broke.

The lumbering vehicle began rolling backward, and the brakes
weren't strong enough to stop it. On the left side of the truck was a
deep ravine three or four hundred feet down. On the other side of
the trail was the mountainside. All I could do was turn the wheel
into the mountain, but as the truck went into the loose soil on the
sloping mountain, it rolled up, and flipped upside down on its top.

It seemed to be moving in slow motion. Just up and over, and
then *kerplunk* on its top. The little boy in front with us started howling.
His mother was more concerned with him than herself. Transmission
fluid started dripping down on Marilee and was running through
her hair and down her face. We crawled out as quickly as we could
to survey the damage.

First we accounted for the passengers who had been riding in the back. There were some bumps and bruises, but the boys were all right. Except Jimmy wasn't there. Marilee and I looked at each other and froze for a moment. He had been riding right behind the cab, which was now flat. If our six-year-old son was under there, he wouldn't have a chance. With a queasy feeling in the pit of my stomach I bent down and looked under the truck.

There, swinging back and forth by his belt, arms flailing, was our son. As the truck turned over he must have gotten caught on a bolt, and he was now hanging from the bottom of the truck, his head just inches from a big rock. If his belt had not got hooked up like that, his skull would have been crushed. I got him loose, he crawled out and got a good deal of hugging.

We stood there in the middle of the trail and praised the Lord—an impromptu prayer meeting on the side of a mountain.

Before long Pop Weaver's son came along and found us blocking the road. He hooked his cable onto the truck and pulled it upright. Naturally, we had a spare axle along in case we needed it to pull ourselves out of a mud hole. That happened to be just the spare part we needed, so we changed the axle while Dave Spare hiked up and got some water for the radiator. I hooked the battery back up, turned the key, and she cranked right up. We loaded all the stuff back in and proceeded to the lake and the children who were waiting for Christmas.

An experience like that makes you pause and consider just how fragile life is. Here we were living in a situation where we were constantly hearing of raids and attacks on surrounding villages, yet we could all have been killed in that truck accident. There is no real place of safety for any of us, but you can't accomplish anything if you are living in constant fear. You have to put your trust in the Lord and go on with the tasks He has assigned you. Fleeing to a place of supposed security is useless. The safest place for any Christian is in the center of God's will.

As 1972 turned into 1973 tensions grew. We didn't feel in any danger, but just across the boundary in the adjoining province we could often hear shell fire and the roar of cannons. Hundreds of evacuees poured into our town from these areas. They came with no food, shelter, or employment and taxed the facilities in Marbel.

Rumors ran everywhere about ambushes and raids. There were never any official confirmations or denials, but the evacuees told harrowing stories. In Lutayan, one of the small towns about six miles northeast of us, thirteen Ilongos were massacred. The bodies were brought into the municipal building, creating a sensation. Because this was a Moslem community the government forces burned down the whole village as an example to the rebels who had killed the two families.

This completely emptied the community, sending more evacuees fleeing for their lives with only what they could carry with them. This also created a gutted-out no man's land about five miles wide from there to Marbel. Any buildings that they couldn't burn were riddled with bullets, leaving a totally devastated area that was soon overgrown with weeds.

Similar occurrences in many nearby communities discouraged people from planting crops. One American who had invested a great deal of money trying to create a sound agricultural project in that area decided to give up. We were able to lease one hundred hectares of his land for a very reasonable sum and began farming the land, which was about six miles north by northwest of us. That wasn't as foolhardy as it might sound, for at least it was closer to Marbel and didn't require long periods of driving where I had to go through so many checkpoints. I wasn't concerned about going into Moslem territory, because we had always had good relations with them. There were a number of Moslem students in our schools by this time, and there was no discrimination in their treatment.

No sooner had we planted the fields with *milo* than another problem cropped up. Squatters, former employees of the American fellow, moved onto the land without permission and tried to claim ownership. Because the land was under lease they had no right to claim it for land reform, but it was an unpleasant situation. These people were very much at enmity with us, and we felt rather sorry for them. They had no other place to go, but they couldn't just claim the land we were legally leasing from its proper owner. Besides we were in desperate need for the profit the crops would bring.

Then early one morning one of our farmworkers came running to our home, his face ashen with fear. "They've killed the squatters! It's a massacre!"

"Calm down, Jaime. Tell me exactly what happened."

"Just before dawn a band of rebels, Black Shirts, came to the squatters' shacks, probably just seeking food. One of the squatters shot at them, and the rebels opened fire. At least a dozen squatters, women and children too, are dead. As many more were taken off as captives. They killed all the men and kidnapped the rest of the women."

"Get in the truck. We'll go see for ourselves."

"Oh, Jerry, do you think you should go out there?" Marilee protested.

"The authorities are out there by now. I'll be perfectly safe, but this happened on land we are leasing, and it is generally known that those folks considered us enemies. I want to make certain the army knows we had nothing to do with this."

"Oh, that's right," she agreed. "It does look bad for us, doesn't it? We wanted them off the land, and now they are gone."

I went and officially registered our innocence, but there were still people in the district who were suspicious of us. There was an investigation, and of course none of the evidence pointed in our direction, but it was an uncomfortable situation.

The bombings and shellings went on and on and on. There would be a rebel raid, and people would be killed, then the army would move in and kill more people, then the rebels would take revenge. There were horrible stories of atrocities on both sides, but I'd rather not repeat them. The situation was getting very discouraging.

Also the Hibschmans' term was up, and their leaving was sorely felt. They had done a tremendous job, and we really hated to see them go. He's now pastoring a C&MA church in New Jersey, but we'd still welcome them back any time they wanted to come.

We were really having difficulties getting teachers with the degrees required by the new ordinances. Trying to help the evacuees was a drain on our rather meager resources. To add to our problems we had a severe drought, and our crops were nothing to brag about.

You'd think that with the sounds of war in the background the other problems would fade into the distance, but they don't. Often the minor irritations add up and are more discouraging than major calamities. I'll have to admit I was really feeling down.

Then a letter came from Tito DeGuzman. The DeGuzman family were some of our earliest friends in Manila after we began renting their house during our first term in the country. We'd never lost contact with them and would often visit with them when we were in the capital. They were so good to us that one time Marilee commented, "I hope they don't feel they are going to earn their way into heaven by being so kind to us. They just can't seem to do enough for us."

I tore open the envelope and began to read the seventeen-page letter. Before I was two pages into it, the tears were streaming down my face. He went on and on about how his whole family had come to know the Lord through our witness. He told about all his brothers and sisters who were now serving the Lord. He told how much our friendship had meant to them, how they respected us and were grateful to us.

I can't express how much that letter meant coming at that time. All of a sudden any inconveniences we faced seemed insignificant. The letter was a reminder that it wasn't our work but the Lord's, and even if we were killed His work would go on. There was nothing to fear. God is still sovereign.

With tragedies happening all around us it was remarkable that our town had not yet been a place of battle. Every other community seemed to have problems with the Moslem Black Shirts, but we remained a neutral island in the raging sea of rebellion.

Of course there were pessimists who kept warning us that it was just a matter of time. Our turn would surely come. Perhaps that was the reason no one was surprised when word came that the rebel forces were advancing into Marbel. No one came to the office to give official warning; the messenger just ran to the classrooms shouting, "The rebels are coming! They are crossing the river at the ferry and are coming this way!"

The river crossing is only about a mile from the campus, so everyone panicked. Students and teachers alike began to run. It was pandemonium—people running, crying, fleeing toward the center of town, carrying whatever they could. Parents dashed onto campus frantically searching for their children.

Word came to the radio station, and the staff immediately went off the air, closed the station, and ran. One teacher ran barefoot past me toward the town square. I kept trying to calm people down, but no one would listen. It seemed so illogical to all run to one central place. That would just make it easier on any force that was trying to wipe out the population. I felt certain the safest thing would be for all to go to their homes, but I couldn't make myself heard.

I tried making an announcement over the public address system, to no avail. I didn't know what else to do, so I began playing inspirational music, hoping that would calm everyone down, but nothing helped. Shortly the campus was completely vacant. It was eerie, as if the rapture had come, and I was the only one left.

I walked across campus and crossed the road to our house. Even the guard had left his post. There was no one on the street, and the quiet was unreal. Even the dogs stopped barking.

"Daddy, Daddy! I saw a man in a black shirt coming up the road!" Jimmy yelled as I walked into our house. His eyes were wide with fear.

"Oh, son, they're called Black Shirts, but they don't all really wear black shirts. It was probably just a coincidence that you saw someone dressed in black."

Marilee was very quiet and subdued. "Do you think they are really coming?" she asked.

"I don't know. It seems as if they should be here by now. I do know that running to town won't help us. The safest thing for us to do is stay right here. They don't have any argument with us."

We sat there waiting. Praying. I kept thinking about different members of our staff, wondering where they were and what they were doing. Later I got to talk to some of them and pieced together the scenario.

"I was walking to town to deposit some money in my grandson's account," Mr. Llobrera told me. "I observed people were running. I was wondering why their movements were so fast, when I heard some one cry, 'The Moslems are coming!'

"I didn't know what to think. Then when I arrived at the bank, the manager was closing it. He was going to run, too. All the shops were closing, and more and more people were running into the square, trying to get on buses going anywhere. All the yellow buses were packed."

"Our little girl, Fae, ran in from school and began packing her clothes," Romeo Mojica recalled. "I felt we would be safer in our home, so we did not run."

"I was at the radio station," Avelina Cargas said. "We remembered how the rebels in another city had occupied the radio station and broadcast over it, so we took the crystal, and we all ran. My baby was in my home and my little children, and I ran to them as fast as I could. When I get there I began packing food and clothes in a basket. We were so frightened. From now on, I will keep a basket packed just in case."

"I felt we were safest in our home," her husband, Pete, added. "I packed a suitcase and waited for instructions."

The stories went on and on. Everyone remembered just where he was and what he was doing when he heard the news. When the story proved to be just a rumor, everyone was embarrassed. In the town square the municipal officials went around with loud speakers shouting, "Go home. There is no attack. Return to your homes."

The reaction to the rumor showed just how tense everyone was. The constant sounds of bombing and strafing only miles from us affected everyone's nerves. In a way the panic was a blessing. It released the fears people had been holding back and made them more careful about rumors in the future.

Discussing the incident with our staff later, we were able to make plans in case a real attack should take place. "The market would be the first place to be attacked," I emphasized. "The campus would probably be the safest because it is peaceful, and the rebels would not be attacking children. If any more such rumors come, stay in your classrooms, keep the children calm, and wait for further instructions."

One of the teachers, who had a daughter about to graduate, was still so terrified that she refused to remain until graduation. She and the girl left for Ilo-Ilo City. Many of the townspeople were slow to return. I don't know where they thought they would be safer. As news of all the troubles was finally released to the rest of the nation, Mindanao get a very bad reputation. Whenever I went to Manila on business, people would ask, "Are you going back?" and, "It is too dangerous in Mindanao. How can you return?"

I didn't consider myself particularly brave by returning. Matter of fact, I felt safer, more relaxed, in Marbel than I did in Manila. I guess I was learning the truth the psalmist had expressed so well: "The Lord is the strength of my life; of whom shall I be afraid?"(Psalm 27:1).

"You know there is a real question as to whether the military is going to be able to control the rebels or not," my American visitor said. "There could be a real takeover. A revolution."

"Oh, I don't think there is any danger of that yet, Jack," I replied. Jack was a US AID man who was spending the night at the Barker Hotel. It is always good to have a chance to talk with folks from home, and he preferred staying in a private home when he was in town. His job was promoting farm crops, grain sorghum in particular, so we had a common interest. He had been out of the area for some time and had come to spend a day or two surveying the territory and checking up on some of his projects.

"Jared, all Peace Corps and AID personnel carry airplane tickets on their person at all times."

"Oh, I know some missionaries that carry open-dated tickets with them, too. I really think that is useless. An open-dated ticket means you have no reservation. If anything big happened, they couldn't get out of here anyhow. The airport would be swamped. No one would get out of Surallah. So why bother?"

"Well, just what is your plan of action in case of a rebel attack in Marbel?" he persisted.

"Oh, we're sort of banking on the embassy to inform us if there is any need to evacuate."

At this he threw back his head and laughed a long, hearty, knee-slapping laugh. "Oh, Jared," he finally explained, shaking his head. "Don't you realize the embassy gets its information from me? And I get my information from folks like you?"

I was a little nonplussed to learn that, but I replied defensively, "Well, we do have an airstrip here at King's. We also have radio connections with the Baptist base at Malaybalay, and we've made a point to stay in touch with them every day during these times. If there is anything really touchy going on here, we can ask them to monitor us all day. They could contact Wycliffe to send a plane down here to get us in an hour's time if we were in real danger."

That seemed to reassure him some, and he didn't press his point any further during his visit.

We were having our annual spiritual emphasis week on our campuses and really didn't have much time to consider the advice we had been given. Two evangelists from Ambassadors for Christ International were speaking for us, and the response was beautiful. More than 180, mostly new students, came forward to receive Jesus Christ as Savior. Many of these students were enrolled in the newly opened vocational courses. Their responsiveness seemed indicative of the openness of heart and spiritual hunger of the masses during this time of upheaval.

The next week we were busy setting up a follow-up program for those who had made decisions, when a knock came to our door. Marilee answered and was handed a letter. She opened it and read it. "It's from Jack," she said with a funny look on her face. "He's concerned about us. He says we are not taking the situation seriously enough. That it is very serious."

"It seems strange that he would have a letter hand delivered," I murmured.

"I guess he doesn't trust the mails. He says, 'You better keep your powder dry.' What does that mean?"

"I'm not sure, but I have been thinking about some of the things he told us," I replied.

"Should we go buy plane tickets?" she asked.

"Oh, no. I really believe that would be useless. Besides it would create suspicions and make people more uneasy if they knew about it. You know how the whole population has been eyeing us."

"Well, what then?"

"Oh, just a phrase he used. Remember he said he was getting information from us?"

"Yeah. Oh! You don't think he could be with the CIA or something, do you?"

"I'd never thought about it before, but you know all the talk that's been going around about missionaries being members of the CIA. We've always been friendly with any Americans who come around. Maybe we should be more careful."

"Oh, but I hate to be suspicious of people."

"So do I, but we can't jeopardize our work here."

"That's true," she agreed.

After that we became more aware of how closely people were watching our behavior. If the whole family got in the truck at once, someone was sure to stop by and ask, "Are you coming back?" And they'd check out the truck to make sure we weren't taking our belongings with us.

We made a point of being very casual and tried not to all leave together. Even the staff was somehow banking on our presence. When we took a vacation there were all sorts of rumors. Many of the teachers told us of being asked, "Are the Barkers coming back?"

Then the rumors began that we were CIA. This got so out of hand that even some of our teachers began eyeing us suspiciously. When I mentioned the problem in one of my letters to our board members, one of them wrote our US Senator, Robert Dole, about the problem. The senator issued a statement on his official stationery stating that the US government had not and would not use missionaries as spies.

We could only hope this would convince people, although we could understand their suspicions. We were probably more aware of what was going on than any other foreigners, but this wasn't because we were subversive in any way. We were in touch with the situation because we were in daily contact with the people. We had friends on all sides of the conflict because we tried to remain neutral.

All this controversy made us aware of our greatest fear. Not fear for our physical safety, but that for some reason we might be forced to leave our work. We were there not as representatives of our country, but as ambassadors for Christ.

11
God Is Faithful

Christmas of 1973 marked fifteen years since our arrival in Mindanao. One of our first prayers on beginning the work was that we might have a witness to the Moslem groups on the island. Instead we were now divided from them by a five-mile no-man's land that presented a physical barrier somehow symbolic of the spiritual and cultural barrier that also existed.

This situation was a real burden to me, and I felt compelled to at least make an attempt to do something about it. So one Sunday afternoon Marilee and I drove out through the deserted area toward the town of Lutayan. The desolation of the land that had once been the productive homeland of many families was heartrending.

"Oh, look," Marilee cried just before we neared the town. "There's one woman out there all by herself."

I looked over at the lonely lady silhouetted against the barren background. There was something pitiful about her, yet I had to admire her courage. She was trying to resume her life, to put back the pieces that had been shattered by the senseless destruction of war.

We pulled into the little burned-out town, appalled by the devastation. The area by the municipal building was completely burned. It was surrounded by old hollow block frames. Often there were just a few posts remaining. The market was completely gone. And most eerie of all, there were so few people. This had been a thriving community, and now it looked almost like a ghost town.

I stopped in front of the municipal building, and we got out. This building was covered with pockmarks from submachine guns. Where the bullets had hit, the cement had cracked, and chunks had fallen off. I asked an officer stationed there about the people farther out.

"There are no people in the barrio," he responded.

"Do you think it would be safe for us to visit where the community had been?" I asked.

"No."

"Well, we'd like to go out there. We'd like to see if there is any way we can help the people who lived there."

He was less than enthusiastic but finally agreed to go with us the following day. We couldn't even drive into the place, because the bridge had been destroyed. We got out and crossed the little creek on a log. We found the barrio almost deserted. There were just a handful of people milling about. They had come to trade or buy food, but the fish market was gone. The outsiders from Marbel were afraid to come across no-man's land to buy the fish, and the Moslems were afraid to venture into town. It was a ridiculous situation, for the people were economically dependent on one another, yet because of the fear there was very, very little trading going on.

These people seemed to be in need of everything. Their homes were gone, as was their income from fishing as well as farming. They were, for the most part, innocent victims of circumstances over which they had no control. We wanted to help them. We had wanted to make contact for fifteen years, and this seemed to be the Lord's time. As always, His timing is perfect.

World Vision was sponsoring a Revolution of Love by sending out teams of young people, American and Filipino, four or five to a team. Through our contacts in Lutayan we were able to get a team in there, the only team that did get to work with the Moslems.

Using PEEI trucks, equipment, and men, the team first put in a well and pump. The water was full of minerals, but it was drinkable. Then the housing project began. We provided cogan grass, bamboo, and nipa for the houses, and the team supervised the labor as the villagers pitched in and helped. We plowed five acres and divided off garden spots. We provided seeds so the people would soon be producing food. I was particularly pleased with these projects, because they were helping the people help themselves.

We put in a cement floor, thinking it could be used for playing basketball, so they could have some recreation, but it was soon being used to dry fish and shrimp. The people seemed particularly pleased with the little town hall that was the first building back in the area. It gave them a place to meet. All this takes time, and the team was with us for about ten months—staying in our home, naturally. It was an exciting experience, for we not only had the satisfaction of helping people, but we were also making friends, something that had been impossible all the years we had been praying, waiting on the Lord.

During one of our early visits out there we met a little blind girl named Taya. She was about seven years old and was a victim of the evacuation. She had been sick with measles when her family had to flee to safety, and the infection had gone into her eyes and caused her to lose her sight.

Taya's father was gone. No one knew what had happened to him, but now the mother and children were living with an elderly grandfather. We were touched when they demonstrated their faith in us by allowing us to take the little girl away to the city to be checked by a doctor. The grandfather could speak Tagalog quite well, so I could communicate with him, and he often served as translator for us. Because of our obvious interest and concern in the child he finally told us, "Well, we will just give you Taya. She is your little girl now."

We made arrangements for her to have an operation in Davao, and when she began to see, they decided she was their girl again. Unfortunately, the improvement in her sight was only temporary, and when she began to go blind again, they were ready to give her to us. The best we could do was try to find a school for the blind she could attend.

As our relationship within the community continued to develop we took our old films out there and showed them. Even though most of the people didn't understand English well enough to grasp everything, we hoped they would get the gist of the message. They certainly did enjoy them. The runaway favorite was *Mr. Texas*. They got a big kick out of all those cowboys and whooped and hollered.

Every success seems to bring with it problems, and in this instance it was the suspicions aroused among our Ilongo friends. The rebel movement was continuing, and seeing us going out among their enemies, even helping their enemies, naturally made them wonder about our loyalties. It is difficult to be neutral in such a situation, but we tried walking this very fine line. The various enterprises we had begun over the years were all still continuing, and we tried to make it clear that we loved everyone because of Jesus.

We were just thankful for the reassurance that God does answer prayer—not always when we want Him to, for we are so often impatient, but He does answer.

All kinds of excitment was going on during the days of the Revolution of Love project with the Moslems. Marilee and I were especially pleased with the letters coming from Johnny during his senior year of high school. First there was one that said: "Captain Bob Smithheart of United Airlines is giving flying lessons for only $5 an hour. When I first heard about it that seemed impossible, but it is true. He is just charging for the gas. I'm learning to fly at last."

After that it seemed every letter was filled with stories of flying. "We fly in a Cessna one seventy-two. That's a four-seater, bigger than a two-seater training plane but smaller than the Helio Couriers and Pipers that Wycliffe uses." His graduation seemed anticlimactic for him. The big news was when he received his pilot's license. Then he wanted to come home, that is, to the Philippines, for a year. His mother wasn't too sure about that.

"It's too dangerous. He would be safer in the States."

"Oh, Marilee, things have calmed down considerably. I don't think he would be in any particular danger here."

"We haven't had any attacks in our province for a while, but they are still going on in the surrounding provinces, and who knows when they might break out here again."

"Well, he'll be as safe as we are," I insisted. I was looking forward to having Johnny around for a year. Postponing his college work that lor g wouldn't hurt him, and he was a good worker.

The years when my sons were little tykes and I'd taken them with me to the fields had paid big dividends. All three were proving to be very handy with machinery, and not one was afraid to sweat a little. Seeing my sons grow up, following in my footsteps, made me understand better how my own father had felt about his three sons. I could sympathize with his dream of a family farm where all his boys could work side by side and how hard it was for him when I "deserted" him by coming to the mission field.

As pleased as I was with my boys, I'll have to admit that my old buddy Richard Spare had been doing some excellent training of his boys back on the farm in Kansas. After David Spare's year of service was up he recruited his next brother, Dan, to come out and take his place. We not only appreciated all the work they did, but also the fact that their keen interest in all we were doing in Mindanao was a good indication that the Spare family had been praying for us all these years, almost as if the Barkers have been a family project for them.

I was in Manila on business when Johnny arrived from the States. "Your mother and I have been debating whether you ought to come out or not," I admitted to him. "But we think it is safe enough."

"Good!" he exclaimed. He couldn't have cared less if it was safe or not. He just wanted to come home.

"One of the top men in the Philippine constabulary was ambushed a couple of weeks ago, and that has created a bit of unrest in Marbel, but we had already given you permission to come. So—"

"Oh? Really?" he replied nonchalantly. "Let me tell you about getting my pilot's license. Paul Carlson was in Seattle taking helicopter training, and the day I had my check ride I got to see him and tell him I'm a pilot now, too."

"Well, that was quite a coincidence, seeing someone from the Phiippines."

"Yeah. He's one of the first Wycliffe pilots I ever flew with. It was really neat having him there that day. Almost like family."

John became totally involved with all that was going on, just as I knew he would. He was elected president of the young people's group at church, played the new guitar we'd given him for graduation for various youth groups and on the radio. I put him to work on the latest building project on the campus, a much-needed auditorium. This was just a rectangular cement-block builing with a stage on one end, but it was impressive to us, since it would seat 500.

When the building was nearing completion a thirty-five-night evangelistic campaign was planned. Services would be held in every little town in the area ending with a week of meetings held in the new auditorium and broadcast over DXKI. Jim Prieto, the well-known Filipino evangelist, preached. Luni Lahaylhay was the featured soloist, three young men from Bob Jones University had special music, and we'd show a film. The services would often last three hours, but that was according to local custom, and no one complained. Doing this every night wore me out, but it was worth it. The Lord answered years of prayers by sending a real, heaven-sent revival. The response was beyond our expectations, and the people turned out night after night to hear the gospel. We recorded nearly 2,000 decisions.

John considered the crusade the highlight of his year home. As far as I know, he was the only one who attended every single night.

He was the official sound man and projectionist and had to set up the equipment each night and then take it down afterwards. The main problem with this was the midnight curfew that was still in effect. He only missed it one night when the truck got stuck in a big mud hole. Thankfully the soldiers who stopped him knew who he was, and they let him go.

An added bonus to having the three BJU students staying with us was they kept telling John about the mission aviation course offered at Bob Jones. He listened but didn't seem too enthusiastic about enrolling in college. John's the kind of young man who prefers being hot, sweaty, greasy, and working at full tilt to sitting in an air conditioned classroom wearing a coat and tie.

Shortly before leaving for furlough at the end of his year with us, I came down on him pretty hard about school. "You'd better start getting your applications in," I instructed him. My kids all can tell when I really mean something, and I seldom have to say a thing twice. Two weeks after we returned to the States he enrolled in the missionary aviation course as an advanced student, since he already had his pilot's license.

It might be a sign of old age creeping up on me, but furlough years seem to come faster than they used to, and they go quicker. We've developed a pattern to our lives during our time in the States. Our main purpose is to update our supporters on what is going on in Mindanao, and this keeps us on the road a good deal. Having an opportunity to be with our family and to fellowship with old friends is a special blessing.

I've also become a bit of a scavenger. There are a lot of bargains to be had from surplus stores, auctions, going-out-of-business sales, and the like, if you really work at it. And I do. We try our best to stretch the dollars that are donated for equipment. My father pitched in again during '75 and helped in finding and procuring much of the supplies and equipment we were to take back with us to the field.

The time I got to spend with my father was especially precious, for he was eighty-seven years old, and his strength was failing, even though he wouldn't admit it. He still lived alone, drove his car, and raised dahlias. He had fifty varieties and could name every one of them. His flowers were his joy in his old age, and he supplied floral arrangements for all weddings and funerals in the community.

Bill Barker was a good man, and I was proud to be his son. I've often heard that the hardest people to win to Christ are those in your own family, and I believe it. How could I convince him that he was a sinner, that Christ had come to seek and to save those who are lost? All I could do was continue to pray.

We had a very special send-off in Seattle that year. Both my sisters were there with my dad, who had made the trip to the Coast for the occasion. We were looking forward to the next term, in spite of the pressures of living under martial law. The Lord isn't hindered by minor inconveniences like that. We had seen so many answeres to prayer, and before the next term was over Johnny would have finished his education, and we'd have our own pilot on the field.

The bed rocked me awake. "Jared, it's an earthquake!" Marilee shouted.

"It sure is." As we fought to crawl out of the shaking bed, I yelled, "Jabe!" Since the walls in our house don't go all the way to the high vaulted ceiling, he had no trouble hearing me.

"I—I'm coming, Dad."

The three of us struggled to get to the front door, hindered by the rolling of the floor. It felt as if we were on a sailboat in a stormy sea. We had no sooner made it down the front stairs when the railing toppled over. "Let's hang onto the gate," I yelled.

It was midnight, pitch dark, which made the sounds all the more terrifying. The quake sounded like a freight train in the distance. All the neighborhood dogs were barking, and we could hear people shouting back and forth. Tin roofs were making cracking noises, and there was a constant rattling sound.

We just stood there hanging on to the gate posts. It was impossible to stand without holding on to something. It had happened so suddenly that it took a while to shake off the feeling that I was still asleep. That first quake lasted probably four or five minutes, but it seemed much longer. When the shaking settled down we made our way back into the house. The electricity was off, so we didn't even try to check for damage but went back to bed. Before I was asleep again an aftershock began. This went on the rest of the night.

When the sun finally rose we rolled out and began checking for damage. The refrigerator was about two yards from the wall. The piano had moved, but hadn't tipped over. Things were topsy-turvy all over the house, but nothing appeared to be broken. I opened a cupboard door, and dishes came tumbling out and some of them broke, the only damage upstairs.

Downstairs I checked the concrete posts that held the house up. Every one had a crack. Some had broken away from the cement blocks that were supposed to keep them from dropping.

Across the road I could see that the back wall of our new auditorium was cracked from top to bottom. I hurried over and inspected the building, but that was all the damage I found. In the administration building, which is one of the original buildings on campus, tables, typewriters, and books were spilled all around, but the building was still standing.

Art Pabellyon, the station manager for DXKI, came in just as another aftershock began. "Have you gotten any news?" I asked.

"I heard that Cotabato City was the hardest hit. Evidently the epicenter of the quake registered eight on the open-ended Richter Scale. That's a big one."

"I believe it."

We talked a bit about how we could be of service in the rescue work that would be needed in the hardest hit areas. A special government agency was being set up to organize the relief work, so we contacted them. It took a couple of days to straighten up in Marbel, then Art, Jabe, and I took a bus to Cotabato City on the eastern coast of the island. Because the direct road to the city was still closed by the rebels, we had to take a roundabout way, and it took us all day to travel the 100 miles to Cotabato City.

We spent the night with Art's parents outside the city and the next morning continued our trip. As we neared the city the bus stopped, and the driver announced this was as far as he could go. The two-lane, 100-yard long concrete bridge was out. We got out and walked to the river. One section of the bridge had shaken loose from its pillars and was sitting down in the water.

We took a boat across the river and entered the heavily damaged city. I was glad I'd thought to take my camera along, because the quake had left some crazy-looking destruction. One four-story apartment building kind of collapsed down into itself. There were hotels that looked as if one or two stories had sunk into the ground. One building next to a church was leaning so that only the church was keeping it from falling over.

It was quite overwhelming. We talked with some government officials, offering to help any way we could, and they put us on helicopters to assist in doing a survey. They had some medicines on board, so we landed in a number of places down the coast and dropped off the supplies. The coast was absolutely wiped out. The whole coastline, which had been lined with coconut trees and houses, was a bare sandbar. There was no way to tell how many people had been swept out to sea by the 18-foot tidal wave that followed the quake.

We came back and arranged for people in Manila to ship supplies to the area—tents, prefabricated houses, all kinds of relief goods. Many Christian organizations were helping, including World Vision, World Concern, and FEBC. The National Disaster Coordinating Center came up with a casualty report that listed 3,103 persons dead, 2,282 missing, and 28,716 homeless. I don't know how accurate those figures are, but they give an indication of the scope of the problem.

On one of the trips delivering relief goods, I decided to check out an area where they had relocated some Moslem families who had to evacuate because of the rebels. I hoped I might get some word of Badawi. It had been years since we had had any contact with him, and we didn't even know if he was still alive.

I pulled up to the place and asked a passerby if he knew the family. "Why, the father is just in that house right there," he replied. I could hardly believe it. I got out of the truck and walked about three houses down the path, wondering if the father would remember me. I didn't know him very well. He came out and threw his arms around me. "You are our daddy!" he said in his limited English. "We are so glad you came back to see us. I'll send someone for Badawi."

He got a young man to run the two or three miles back into the hills to get Badawi. The family was very cordial to me while I was waiting and brought me some fresh coconut to eat but didn't invite me into the house. These people had almost nothing and were ashamed to ask me into their humble little nipa house. The father was telling me of some of their experiences during the rebellion when I heard the pounding of footsteps on the soft earth. I looked up and there came Badawi, running as hard as his short legs would carry him. It was a big thrill to see him alive.

He gave me such a hug! "Oh, sir, I am so happy to see you again. We had many hard times, and I did not know if we would ever meet again.

"Sir, I need a Bible. I lost mine during the evacuation, and I have a son now, and I want to teach my little boy the Scriptures."

Naturally I promised to get him a new Bible. Moreover, PEEI had inherited from John Sycip a 100-acre farm that was in an isolated area not far from the evacuation center. It was standing idle because it was unsafe for us to get back in there, but Badawi and his Moslem relatives were ecstatic when I asked if they would like to move to that land and work the farm for us. It's rather strange how circumstances work together sometimes—almost as if Someone were directing us.

It was also because of our involvement in the relief program that we came in contact with World Concern. When I learned that Art Beals, the founder of World Concern was flying into Davao, I drove over to meet with him. I was staying with a Conservative Baptist missionary, Bob Scivington, who was also a friend of Mr. Beals. While we were talking we were joined by a young Filipino doctor named Rene Sison, who also had an appointment with Art Beals.

The four of us went out to eat, and Art and Bob got to talking about old times, leaving Rene and I sitting there looking at each other. This proved to be quite a blessing. It took Doc and me about five minutes to discover we were kindred spirits. "I've worked in mission hospitals ever since I graduated," he told me. "Every opportunity I get, I fly with missionaries back into the tribal barrios to preach and check the patients. My heart is really with the tribal peoples."

"Well, we have a school for the T'Bolis up at Lake Sebu, and we've been wanting to start some kind of a medical outreach for them ever since we began up there, but we lack the personnel."

"I'd love to work in a situation like that, but it takes money for land, buildings, equipment. I'm here to talk to Art Beals about a medical mission organization of Filipino doctors and nurses, called Medical Ambassadors of the Philippines. World Concern is thinking of supporting us."

"But at Lake Sebu PEEI already has land and buildings. We might even be able to get some help with equipment. We need personnel. Maybe—"

We looked at each other for a minute, smiled, then laughed. We were both thinking the same thing. I invited him to come visit us and promised him a trip to Lake Sebu, and he accepted. I was so excited. Another answer to prayer. Again, it hadn't happened right when I wanted it, but I felt certain this was the beginning of a new missionary medical program.

Art Beals and I flew from Davao, on the southeastern coast of Mindanao, over the mountains to the eastern coast city of Cotabato in a little Cessna. During the trip we got to talk, and this marked the beginning of PEEI's relationship with World Concern. As we crossed the rugged mountains in Manobo territory, I looked out my window and said, "Art, this is our next target area. We are determined to reach those people somehow."

On our return trip the pilot refused to fly back over the mountains. "No. I've been talking to some other pilots, and they say it is too dangerous. There are many rebels in the mountains, and they like to shoot at planes. Some have powerful machine guns, and they could hit us."

So we flew around the south coast of the island. "If it is as dangerous in Manobo territory as the pilot says, are you sure you want to go back in there?" Art asked.

"Oh, I don't think it's all that bad. People tend to exaggerate. If I can get government approval, we'll make a survey in the area the first of the year."

"Well, if you're willing to go, I imagine World Concern will help fund the project."

That was all the encouragement I needed. Permission to travel in the area was granted by an official who made it clear he had strong doubts about my mental condition. A group of us struck out in the four-wheel-drive truck. Tim Wilbeck and Randy Evans, the short-termers who replaced Dan Spare and my sister Lillian; Sam Lobore, one of our schoolteachers who was from that area to serve as our guide; Pastor Napilo from Lake Sebu, since he spoke T'Boli, and I'd been told the Manobo are somewhat familiar with that language; my fifteen-year-old son, Jabe; and myself.

We started out with intentions of going to a little community named Masiag, but our guide didn't know which fork in the road to take to get there, and by the time we realized we were on the wrong road, we couldn't backtrack. The road was so muddy there was no chance of backing out, and there was no room to turn around, so we just kept going.

The muddy logging road was as bad as any I'd ever seen, but the scenery was beautiful. We kept sliding along, crossed through a picturesque river, and finally made it to a settled area called Camp Three. We asked around for any Manobo that might be living there, and to our great surprise Mr. DePadro, the father of one of our students at Kalawag, came running up to us.

"Oh, you ought to have a school here!" he exclaimed when we told him of our mission. "We are looking for someone to help us start a church."

After talking with him a while we discovered that we were much closer to Kulaman, the place where we had picked up the boy with the fruit bats, than if we had taken the right turn when we'd started into the mountain area. We got some rather vague instructions of how to reach a Manobo village and took off driving across the fields. The going wasn't any worse than the road had been, and we finally found the house we were looking for. From there we were supposed to take an hour's hike up a steep mountain grade.

We talked to the fellow who lived in the house and got permission to leave the truck parked there. "We'll be spending the night up the mountain," I explained, "but we'll be back here about nine o'clock tomorrow morning. If there are any Manobo who are interested, we'll hold a worship service here then."

The "hour's hike" turned into a three-hour test of endurance, and it was after dark when we reached the settlement. The boys all made it fine, but I realized I wasn't as young as I used to be. The barrio captain in the little community that was named Kulaman invited us to spend the night with him. So we had a bamboo floor to sleep on that night.

The next morning we talked to the captain, and he informed us, "There aren't too many Manobo right here, but if you will climb up the mountain another hour or so—" I really wasn't interested in climbing too much more.

The way back down the mountain was quite steep. There was no trail, and in places we had to fight our way through the brush, across cornfields, and over fallen trees. I'd never been as good a hiker since I'd taken that medicine for snail fever, and as bad as it hurt my pride, I had to admit I was just plain worn out.

A couple of the men who had accompanied us went down and got a horse for me to ride the rest of the way. I was not only tired physically, but my spirits were low. After all the years I'd dreamed about coming back into these mountains to reach the Manobo, now I couldn't even find them. I don't remember when I felt more discouraged than when I was clinging to the little mountain pony, making our way down the mountain.

We had expected to be back to the truck by nine o'clock, but it was eleven when we neared the place, and I looked up. There was a crowd of Manobo waiting for us. We were about two hours late, but around 200 of the tribespeople were standing there waiting patiently. It was so impressive. Such a touching scene, I still tear up thinking about it. Here we'd been searching everywhere, looking all over for Manobo, trying to reach them, and there they were, waiting for us.

We got up on the balcony of the little bamboo house and had a two-hour service. Pastor Napila shared the gospel with them, then explained we were looking for a place to minister to the Manobo. He told them we wanted to help them with their sicknesses, have a school, and teach them agriculture. They were elated.

He closed by saying, "Let's pray now and ask Jesus to help us." I've never seen such a respectful group of pagans in all my life. They all squatted down, flat-footed. The mothers gathered their children to them. Every one of them closed their eyes, and we prayed.

Immediately after the service Datu Aya came to us and said, "The real place to meet Manobos is over in our place—Lagubang." The road to that area had only been open about a week, but we back-tracked until we found it and then drove up the four or five miles to Lagubang. The going was slow, but when we got there, we were on top of the world. We could see all the way to Mount Matutum, the volcano fifteen miles southeast of Marbel. It looked like heaven up there.

We had to return home, but we promised them we would be back. The work among the Manobo had begun at last.

Before the coming of the rainy season in the spring of 1977 we made a number of trips back to Lagubang gathering information so we could make a proposal to World Concern. We'd take along whatever medicine we had on hand, for it seemed 100 percent of the Manobo had something wrong with them. Pastor Napila began making regular trips to get things organized, as we were raising funds for a permanent work there.

The opening of that opportunity seemed like the ultimate realization of answered prayer, but a letter came that summer that was even more impressive. Felipe Fernandez was studying in the States, preparing himself to take over the administration of King's College. He wrote us about going with Johnny and Tim Wilbeck and Randy Evans, who were also back in the States, to visit my father. "I played music for him on a leaf," Felipé wrote. "Then Johnny played his guitar, and we all sang for him. Tim started witnessing to him, and we all talked from the Bible. I shared my testimony with him, and he started to cry. We all surrounded him and put our arms around him, and he prayed and accepted Christ as his Savior. Then we all cried together."

Praise God! Not many men come to Christ in their old age, and the fact that the Lord had seen fit to work through my son, two young men who had been on the field with us, and one of our Filipinos seemed especially significant. This was the sweetest answer to prayer ever.

12
Servants for Christ

The stationery told me the letter was from Wycliffe, but I was unprepared for the message it contained:

"Because of the intensity of the problems in the surrounding areas, the leadership here at Nasuli has been doing some planning about possible evacuation of the Center in the event that it became a necessity. . . We plan to evacuate all of our members to either the Del Monte strip or the Cagayan Airport—depending upon whether we would be using commercial or US Military transport. . . What do you wish us to do for your son, Jimmy, in the event we must evacuate Nasuli?"

My first thought was *These folks are overreacting,* but then I recalled that many of the members had been reassigned to the Philippines after Vietnam had fallen. It's hard for me to consider a takeover of this country I had adopted, yet they knew from experience that it can happen. My next reaction was a sense of gratitude that they were looking out for my son's welfare.

We had been living under martial law for so long we were rather used to the restrictions. We were determined it wasn't going to keep us from going forward in the work, so we began planning a working camp among the Manobo. We'd made a number of overnight trips back to Lagubang, but this was going to be a big project.

Doc Sison was invited to come for the nine-day camp and be in charge of the medical division. He arrived in Marbel at the appointed time, all dressed up in a white *barong tagalog* shirt. While he did look

145

quite professional, that wasn't exactly the correct apparel for camping out in the mountains. We found some clothes for him to wear and teased him a good deal about being so citified. He just laughed. One of the first things I admired about Doc was his sense of humor. That's a real necessity on the mission field.

There were about twenty of us going on this trip—teachers and some students, Jabe, Doc, and I. Marilee was to keep in touch with us by transceiver. We loaded all our supplies, working materials, medicines, garden seeds, and staff into the big truck and hit the muddy trail.

Each day we divided into four areas of ministry. Jabe and I were in charge of the construction team that was building a bunkhouse. This was to serve as an all-purpose building until we could put up a regular classroom building for the school we planned. Because there is very little bamboo at that altitude we brought along a chain saw and sliced lumber out of logs. The roof was to be of grass and the floor of bark stripped from the large trees.

The Manobos realized we were making something permanent and became very enthusiastic. Until that time I don't think they were really convinced we were going to establish a work among them. They became involved in the construction and would do anything they could to help. Real teamwork developed that was extremely encouraging.

We tried to rotate the Manobos so that different ones were on the construction crew each day, because they were the ones who got to ride in the truck. That was a big thing for them. It was interesting to see them inspecting the headlights. They couldn't figure how the light got out of those glass globes.

While this was going on, Doc was having a medical clinic each morning. He treated hundreds and hundreds of patients who came from miles around. Others on the team would gather the patients who were waiting their turns and teach them a bit about agriculture— how to plant vegetables that were lacking in their diets. We distributed seed for them to take home and plant.

After the morning's work we would sit everyone down. Pastor Napila would teach some Bible truths in T'Boli, and that would be interpreted. This took awhile, but it was very effective. They listened so intently.

In the afternoons, during traditional siesta time, we would have Bible study for the staff members. About the middle of the week we

were all stuffed into the uncompleted bunkhouse because it was
raining. We sat around the walls and let our feet dangle in the holes
in the floor. It was still pouring down when Bible study was over, so
we decided to have testimonies. That was going fine until Mr. Napila
spoke, and he really broke up the meeting.

"I feel very convicted," he said. "Here we are having three meals
a day, and we are among these people, many of whom aren't even
eating one meal a day. What kind of testimony is that to them?"

Some of the kids said, "Why don't we share what we have and just
trust the Lord to feed us?"

"Wait a minute," I interrupted. "We brought just enough rice for
us. If we are going to share, then we should be prepared and ready
to sacrifice. We won't be able to go back to the lowlands for more."

They all agreed. "OK, whatever rice we have on hand, we will
distribute it to the Manobo so they can eat with us. That will mean
we will be short a hundred-pound sack of rice."

We began sharing, trusting the Lord to provide for us. The next
morning as we were going through the little barrio of Langal on the
way to our daily outreach post, we found a sack of rice. Now, rice is
very scarce up there, and at that season of the year there just isn't
any. Finding a sack we could buy was a lesson in faith to all of us.

We closed out the work camp with a campfire service. This was a
time of testimonies. One by one our staff members stood and said,
"I've really been challenged in my faith"; "I've learned to trust the
Lord more"; "I have a new vision for missions." And they all wanted
to be assigned to work with the Manobos.

The Manobos who were with us around the campfire didn't understand all the words that were said, but many of them stood and
expressed appreciation that we had come. We had intended the camp
to be a blessing for the Manobo, but I think it was an even greater
blessing to those of us who had come to serve.

Before we left the next morning, I noticed Doc Sison talking with
Datu Aya through an interpreter.

"Do you Manobos know other people?" Doc asked.

"Yes. The T'Bolis."

"Do you know that you and I are both on the island of Mindanao?"

"No."

"Do you know that we are both Filipinos?"

"No."

"Have you heard the name *President Marcos* before?"

"No. We Manobos are blind. But if you show us, we will be able to see. We Manobos are deaf, but if you tell us, we will be able to hear."

A Macedonian call if I've ever heard one.

My father's health had been failing, and when he sent word he wanted to see me I scheduled a trip to Kansas immediately after the completion of the Manobo work camp. I flew to Manila and put in a call to my brother Lawrence to tell him when to expect me. "I've been trying to reach you," he informed me. "Dad passed away three hours ago. He died very peacefully without much pain."

I was disappointed I hadn't been there to tell him good-bye, but I felt at peace about it. He knew I was coming, and that I'd be there for the funeral. After a hectic trip complicated by missing a connecting flight and the fact that I had not even one American dime to make a phone call, I made it to Kansas with just enough time to shower and change before going to the funeral.

John and Felipé were there, and I got to talk to them about my father's profession of faith. The greatest comfort I had was the assurance I'd see him again.

I stayed on for a few weeks so I could spend a little time with my family, my daughters and their families, and John and Felipe. The PEEI board met, and we packed up about $30,000 worth of farm equipment at the Spares' farm. The time was productive, yet I found myself reflecting on how much my father had meant to my life. The older I get, the more I can see some of his traits in myself. I only hope I can pass on some of the values he gave me to my own sons.

One of the Spares' twins, Marlyn, and a friend, Max Meschburger, returned to the Philippines with me. We could always find plenty of work for eager young recruits.

Shortly after we arrived, Mary Weaver died of a heart attack. A very disconsolate Pop came to talk to me. "You know, Mary was a good wife to me," he said. "She was very patient with me, back when I was drinking so much. A good woman. When she got sick, I sold our house and took our savings, about one hundred thousand pesos, and I told her, 'We are going to Manila. Gonna find you a heart specialist.' That made her happy, but it wasn't meant to be. She didn't make it.

"Now my problem is all that money. That's Mary's money. I don't have the heart to spend it. What shall I do with it?"

"How about setting up a Mary Weaver Memorial fund?" I suggested after a bit of discussion. "We could arrange it so that the interest on the money went to scholarships for T'Boli students. That way the capital wouldn't be spent. The fund could continue to send young people to school until the Lord returns."

"I like that!" Pop responded immediately. "A living memorial. Do a lot more good than buying some big marble tomb. She'd like that, too. You know, Jerry, when you become a Christian when you are old, there isn't too much you can do for the Lord. This can make it possible for our witness to live on through the T'Bolis."

Pop didn't realize it, but that statement was comforting to me also. My father had accepted Christ as an old man and didn't have much time to serve the Lord, yet he left five children who could be a witness for him.

Pop dried his eyes, blew his nose, and started shuffling off. "Time to go now," he called. "Dr. McGee's program starts in a few minutes. Can't miss that. He's the best Bible teacher on the air."

The T'Boli New Testament was dedicated soon after this, and that was a thrill for all of us who were concerned about the spiritual welfare of this people. Vivian Forsberg had set out for the Philippines the same time we had, and she and Lillian Underwood, Doris Porter, and Marge Moran had devoted years of their lives to making it possible for the T'Boli to have God's Word in their own language. I really admired them. The Wycliffe folks come as translators and educators, not as missionaries, but the New Testaments they leave behind when their task is finished are invaluable tools to the mission groups who work in the tribes.

Selfishly, I was a bit sad they had finished. First because I'd miss their fellowship as they left the field, but also because that meant there would be no more Wycliffe planes available to us.

Another person who had sacrificed to serve the Lord is Felipe Fernandez. It wasn't easy for him to leave Belen and their little boys, Jay and Joey, to go to the States for two years of study. The government's new regulations stipulated that all schools are to be administered by Filipinos. I believe this is a step in the right direction, but we were put in a difficult position, because it is extremely difficult to find Christians with the dedication the job demands who have the credentials the government requires.

Felipe finished his graduate studies in the spring of 1979 and happily returned to the arms of his waiting family. The separation had been especially difficult for Belen, who was still serving as my secretary. "I had prayed that God would use my husband in His service," she told me. "Then when this opportunity came, I was sad to see him go, but I feel certain it was in the Lord's will.

"It wasn't always easy, for I had to support our sons. One time I had no rice. I prayed for rice for my children. When I dressed for school I felt something in the pocket of my blue skirt. There were a few pesos. Just enough for one *ganta* of rice."

Telling me the story later, she beamed as she recalled the Lord's provision. I had to wonder how many Christians in America would be that thankful for a sack of rice. Her prayer that God would use her husband was also answered. Felipe became dean of the college and administrator of the schools and took on every job that needed doing. He has become a bit of a workaholic, and we now call him "Superservant."

At our next training camp at Lake Sebu we tried an experiment. We selected some of the Manobo to come to the camp with the T'Boli. Just the trip down their mountain, across Allah Valley and up another mountain to T'Boli land was an experience for them. Our purpose was to allow them to see how much more developed the T'Bolis were. We wanted them to realize the value of education and how their lives could be improved.

We had courses in agriculture, health, nutrition, and Bible. The cross-cultural experience proved to be a great success. When the Manobo school was opened shortly after this, everyone wanted to enroll. We had to limit the enrollment to those under twenty-five and still had seventy eager students. Not only did they want to learn to read, but they invited us to have the training camp at Lagubang the next year. They were catching the vision.

A couple of new servants joined the force in Manoboland. Linda Solon was our first nurse in the new clinic, and her teammate, Chris, was a midwife. One of their first goals was to improve the infant mortality rate. There were lots of little babies around, but very few two- or three-year-olds, because so many of them died in infancy. The chance of a newborn's surviving was so slim that the Manobo didn't even name their children until they were old enough that they thought they might survive.

Living at the end of the road, literally, in Lagubang took a good deal of courage for those two young women, especially because the mountains were still filled with rebels. All their concern was for the people they had come to serve.

"How many Manobo are there in this area?" Linda asked.

"About a thousand are within hiking distance."

"And beyond?"

"There are another forty-nine thousand Manobos living in those mountains, who have no access to any kind of medical facilities. No schools. No roads to the outside. There's no way for us to reach them without a plane."

Her gaze went across the lovely green valley stretched out before us to the mountains beyond. "Maybe someday." She smiled.

The "someday" we had waited for so long was coming a step closer. Johnny had finished his course and was doing deputation to raise his support as a full-fledged missionary for PEEI. He even added a new recruit for the task when he married Joyce Calahan, a spunky young lady who was eager to leave the security of Kansas to serve with her new husband in the Philippines. Since she is a nurse, I figured we just might find something to keep her busy.

Having all these people working together toward the goal of reaching those who do not know Christ was exciting. And the excitement grows as the team grows.

John and Joyce arrived on the field in time for their first wedding anniversary. We'd told the staff for a year that they were planning on coming, and Johnny has said all his life this was what he wanted. Still everyone seemed so pleased and proud that they had really arrived. You could hear the whispers:

"Johnny's back!"

"He's one of us."

"He has a Filipina-sized wife."

"He's going to stay and live here, and his first child will be born here."

The firstborn made her appearance on November 9, a dainty little blonde, blue-eyed granddaughter, who was named Angela Sue. She monopolized Joyce and Marilee, but I kept John busy.

It was good to have him back. Whenever there is a job that is too dirty, sweaty, nasty, or just inconvenient, I'll give it to John, and he never complains. Besides, Jabe had discovered electronics by this time and was no longer interested in machines.

Jabe had taken the radio mechanics course at King's and discovered a natural bent. Before long he could fix tape recorders, radios, amplifiers, anything electrical. He worked over at DXKI frequently and picked up a good deal of practical experience. Then he started build-

ing TV antennas and was making money with that. He figured this
would help pay his way to Kansas State, where he wanted to take
the electronic engineering course.

Jim was going to school in Nasuli. Jabe did well with the correspondence courses, but Jim just lacked the discipline to make himself
sit at a desk and study. Not that he is lazy. He always manages to
keep himself busy and would work at the lime factory running the
front loader, or drive a tractor at the farm, or do just anything that
involved machines. Both Jabe and Jim plan to get their education
and return to their home in the Philippines. The thought that all
my boys want to return to the field to help their old dad is a real
encouragement to me.

Another boost came from an unexpected source. Martial law was
lifted in January 1981, so the annual Foundation Day celebration in
Koronadal that February was an especially gay one. The parade was
longer than usual, the bands louder, the floats more festive. It seemed
the whole town turned out for the speeches in the square.

To our surprise, Marilee and I were called to the platform by
Mayor Ischmael Sueno. He began reading an official proclamation:
"By an act of the town council, because your hearts beat as true
Filipinos, and for the work you have done in agriculture and edu-
cation, we hereby proclaim you adopted son and daughter of Ko-
ronadal, South Cotabato, the Philippines." Then he added, "Mr. and
Mrs. Barker, in this day when many are saying, 'Yankee, go home,'
we are saying, 'Yankee, stay! And bring more like you!' "

Being a politician, naturally he spoke longer than that, but that is
the gist of what he said. We were both overwhelmed and so proud
of that proclamation. When you dedicate your life to serving in the
Lord's name, you don't do it to win appreciation or the praise of
men, but if it comes once in a while, it sure is nice.

Then a longtime dream came true. Richard and Neva Jean Spare
came to visit us on the field. After years of supporting us in every
way possible, and even sending three of their boys to help us, they
at last got to visit the land they had prayed for all these years. It was
fun to give them the grand tour of all our projects and to see what
was being done through their eyes.

They were interested in everything that was going on, from the
morning flag raising ceremony at King's, when the student body
prays and sings the national anthem, to sign-off time at DXKI at
night.

"How many people do you think you reach with the radio station?" Richard asked.

"Well, it reaches throughout southern Mindanao, and we've been told there is a potential listening audience of ten million people, but there's no way of telling how many actually listen. Without telephones it's impossible to run any kind of a survey."

We walked around the campus at King's, and he had to inspect the progress on our latest building project—a much-needed library.

"What courses do you offer in the college?"

"B.S. degrees in agriculture, education, and commerce. Or a B.A. Plus the vocational course, secretarial, music education, automotive, electricity, machine shop, refrigeration and air conditioning, and radio mechanics. When Jabe gets back he's planning on adding a course in computers."

"Computers! They have computers in Mindanao?'

"Well, they haven't exactly taken over here as they have in the States, but we have to plan for the future. They're coming, and by the time they become commonplace our students will be prepared to use and repair them."

A trip up to Lake Sebu impressed both Richard and Neva Jean. "It's so beautiful," they exclaimed over and over. The students performed for the Spares, singing and dancing their native dances wearing their colorful, exotic costumes. "What plans do you have for this place?" Richard wanted to know.

"Well, Doc wants the medical clinic to become a training center for village health workers, and before too long we need to begin a high school up here."

"Is this one of the places you'd like to fly into? After coming up that road, I can understand why."

"Oh, that road's in great condition now. You should see it in rainy season. Seriously, it would be great to fly up here, but even if we had a plane we couldn't do that just now—some enterprising farmer has planted corn in the middle of our airstrip."

At Kalawag he was appalled at the condition of the classroom building.

"Well, the bok-bok have been feasting on it awhile," I admitted.

"Bok-bok?"

"An insect. They're not termites, but they do as much damage."

When the principal mentioned they could only have chapel services once a week because there are not enough chairs, and each time they have services all the chairs from the upstairs classrooms have to be moved down and then back again, which is quite a project, Richard muttered, "Something needs to be done about that."

At the agricultural projects near each of the schools he complained, "You're using equipment I'd throw on the scrap heap!"

"We do spend an inordinate amount of time keeping some of these antiques running," I agreed, "but they're all we have." I couldn't help but think, *Well, from now on I'm going to have a friend on the board. Now that he's been here, Richard will understand the situation so much better.*

As we were driving toward the lime factory I explained, "For years this was a losing proposition, but John Sycip insisted we keep at it. If it had been up to me, I'd probably have given up on the lime project, but for the past few years it has kept us afloat financially. When the weather's bad, or for some reason the crops aren't good, we still have a steady income from the lime factory."

In Lagubang the Spares were particularly impressed with the graciousness of the Manobo. "They have been very responsive and appreciative of what we have tried to do for them. Sometimes to a fault."

"How's that?" Richard questioned.

"Well, for example, they gave us a monkey one time. A cute little thing about the size of my fist with a long, long tail. He thought I was his father, I guess, because every evening when I would sit in my favorite chair after supper, and usually fall asleep, he'd come and sit on my shoulder. If I had a toothpick in my mouth, he would pick it out and put it in his mouth. Take his tiny paw and wiggle it all around, just as I did.

"He was a really good pet. Jabe had a drawer in his room that Chip would sleep in. Well, the Manobo found out the Barkers liked that monkey, so they started giving us monkeys! All monkeys aren't that nice to have around, but we didn't want to hurt their feelings when they were trying to please us. At one time we had four monkeys, which is really getting a little much. We finally had to tell the Manobo, 'Thanks, but no thanks.' "

We enjoyed having the Spares around. Before they left, Richard was making lists of equipment we needed, practical things that would expedite the work. "We don't have it that tough," I told him. "At least we don't have to share tea bags anymore as we did in our college days."

The house seemed empty after Richard and Neva Jean left. As I considered how much they had meant to the mission over the years, I concluded that they are as much a part of this ministry as the Barkers are. They've been farming and raising eight kids, but their hearts have always been in missions. We've just had different assignments. They've served in Kansas as we have in the Philippines. Perhaps the unsung heros of faith missions are the folks who stay at home and make it possible for others to go.

When we left for furlough in 1981, we had no worries about leaving the work. After all, Johnny was here. He could take care of everything. Anything he didn't know about running the office, Belen would tell him. We weren't in the States two weeks when Belen had a stroke. This was a blow to the whole staff, for everyone loves Belen. There was never a sweeter, more loving, dedicated woman than Belen Fernandez.

While she was in the hospital, John was in a quandary. He didn't even know where office supplies were kept, and I got a plaintive letter: "Dad, where do you keep the checkbook? I've got to pay everyone and don't have any checks!" We arranged for some long-distance phone calls—the nearest phone to Marbel is forty five minutes away—but it became evident that I'd have to make a return trip for at least a while.

Marilee stayed in Kansas while I returned to straighten things out. "Dad, I never understood just how much pressure you've been under all these years," John said. "I'd always pitch in and help with one project or the other, but I just didn't realize how tough it is to have the responsibility for keeping everything going and everyone happy."

"What's the biggest problem?" I asked after handling the obvious difficulties in the office.

"Lagubang."

"What's going on up there?"

"All kinds of problems. The nurses have been down with really scary stories. The rebel movement is building up again in the mountains, and Juliette, the new nurse, told me about having to run for cover. She and Linda had to hide in the cornfield across the road from the bunkhouse. When she was telling me about it the tears just poured out of her big eyes. 'My bones in me were shaking,' she kept saying, and I didn't know what to tell her.

"Linda was really cool. Her faith is remarkable; she kept telling Juliette, 'The Lord has called us, and He will take care of us.'"

"How are they doing now?"

"The governor has stationed a couple dozen soldiers on the campus, but the nurses seem more afraid of them than reassured by their presence. It really frustrates me," John said, kicking the dust with his foot.

"What do you mean?"

"I wanted to be able to reassure them, tell them, 'Don't worry. I can fly up there in fifteen minutes if there is any danger,' but I can't. It would take half a day to get there, even if we made radio contact, so I knew they needed me."

John doesn't get upset easily, so I realized how bad he felt about not being able to protect those young women.

"What did you tell them?"

"Well, Juliette kept crying, so I just cried with her. I didn't expect her to go back, but the next day in church she got up and gave a testimony. She told the congregation how terrified she is of the sound of bullets, then she went on to say she had been reading John fifteen. She said, 'The Lord reminded me that He had chosen me. Please pray for us as we go back to Lagubang.' They are back there now."

"I'll make a trip up there and check out the situation before I go back to the States," I promised.

John hadn't exaggerated the situation any, but the nurses said they felt at peace staying. "We are needed here," they both insisted. They were more at ease about being in Lagubang than I was about leaving them there. Each morning we talked on the radio at 6:15, which reassured me they were all right, even if talking to me didn't give them any added protection.

On Tuesday morning the week before I was to leave, when I talked to them they were happy and jolly, joking about my acting like a worried father. When I tried to call them the next morning there was no response. I tried again and again. Nothing. I was about to start up there to see if they were all right when a tricycle cab pulled up in front of the house, and there they were.

"Oh, Sir Barker, there was a massacre!" they both told me at once. They were both rather shaky and talking excitedly, so it took me awhile to piece together the story. It seems the massacre had occurred on Monday night in one of the adjoining communities. It took until Tuesday morning, just after I had talked to them, for the wounded to make their way to the clinic.

"Five of our people died!" Juliette wailed.

"No one knows how many died Monday night," Linda added. "They were all shot up, and we were just not equipped to handle all the cases."

"We just bandaged them up and brought them out to the hospital," Juliette interrupted. "They lost so much blood coming down, and there was nothing we could do."

They spent the night and the next morning returned to their post, while I had to leave for the States. I never felt less like leaving.

I had speaking engagements lined up all over the Midwest, and every time I'd tell about those young nurses up in Lagubang, I'd get overcome and just blubber. I'm sure there were people who thought I was overemotional. It's really difficult to explain to Christians in America, who live such nice, easy, comfortable, safe lives, what it is like to live in such a volatile situation.

When our year was up, I was happy to return to the field. The situation in Lagubang remains tense, but when I talked to Juliette again, she said, "The Lord has given me courage to go on. There is no more fear, and I just love this place."

People have different ideas about what constitutes a miracle, but to me, to see the peace this young lady now has when she was so fearful, and with good cause—that's a miracle. Only the Lord can give that kind of peace.

Being back on the field I soon found myself with the same old feeling that I needed to be in ten places at once. In one week a representative from the mayor's office came asking if I could help set up an experimental methane digester project, a farmer came requesting the PEEI join in an agricultural project with a group of his fellow farmers, a Chinese pastor came from General Santos asking that we establish a Christian school in that city, and Doc Sison was running over with new ideas for the medical clinics.

It's as overwhelming as when we began. The more work we do, the more there is. It is impossible to do it all. Yet these opportunities continue to challenge me. It's the little, nitty-gritty, day-to-day problems that discourage me.

Like batteries. We have twelve machines that run off large, heavy-duty batteries, but we only have eight batteries. So every day we switch them back and forth to whatever equipment has priority for that day. My frustration over this problem is compounded by the fact that Jabe made a really great battery recharger before he left for college, a big heavy-duty instrument much better than anything you can buy. Then, while we were in the States, someone plugged in a battery backwards and burned out the charger.

I was just about to sit down to dinner one particularly hot afternoon when one of the men came over to inform me that the electricity was off and they needed a battery to run the generator so the college would have power. I stomped down the stairs and took the battery out of my truck, muttering under my breath, "People who think being a missionary is a glamorous life should see me now."

Lugging the heavy, dirty, greasy battery across the campus didn't seem like the responsibility of a mission executive. "Humph, some big wheel I am. I feel as if I'm four-F in God's army." Then I recalled what my dad had told me so long ago. "We have to pull together to win this war. We each have to do our part. Teamwork, that's what we need."

That's so true. It doesn't matter how important men might think your job is, as long as we work together for the cause of Christ. So I'm just a servant. What greater calling can any Christian have than to be a servant for Jesus Christ?

Moody Press, a ministry of the Moody Bible Institute, is designed for education, evangelization, and edification. If we may assist you in knowing more about Christ and the Christian life, please write us without obligation: Moody Press, c/o MLM, Chicago, Illinois 60610.